Lyman E De Wolf

Money

Its uses and abuses, coinage, national bonds, curency, and banking, illustrated and

explained

Lyman E De Wolf

Money
Its uses and abuses, coinage, national bonds, curency, and banking, illustrated and explained

ISBN/EAN: 9783337114404

Printed in Europe, USA, Canada, Australia, Japan

Cover: Foto ©Suzi / pixelio.de

More available books at **www.hansebooks.com**

MONEY;

ITS USES AND ABUSES,

Coinage, National Bonds, Currency,

AND BANKING,

ILLUSTRATED AND EXPLAINED.

———•◦•———

By LYMAN E. DeWOLF.

———•◦•———

CHICAGO:

PRINTED BY PIGOTT, WEBSTER & CO., 86 & 88 DEARBORN ST.

1869.

PREFACE.

The aim of this work is to furnish for the business and labor-classes a correct outline of our present unjust financial system, as well as an accurate idea of the principles which must be embodied in the national laws to institute a just system. The facts and principles enunciated have been well and fully weighed. The publishing has been more hasty perhaps than was desirable in a work of this importance. The gross and unjust demands of capitalists, coupled with the disordered state of the National finances which their false system has mainly produced, rendered the publication of such a work necessary, and at the earliest possible moment. That there may be some typographical, as well as more grave errors, ought perhaps under the circumstances to be expected. But whatever may be its faults, it is believed, that it substantially sets forth the wrongs of the present system with the remedy to be applied in a manner so plain that it cannot fail to be interesting and useful to all classes of men who desire an honest and uniform currency or money at cost, and thus prefer that right and justice shall be established in the most fundamental law of the nation in place of class inequality and gross injustice.

Under such considerations the work is submitted to the impartial judgment of the American people.

CONTENTS.

CHAPTER IV.

CHAPTER V.

CHAPTER VI.

CHAPTER VII.

CHAPTER VIII.

CHAPTER IX.

CHAPTER X.

CHAPTER XI.

CHAPTER XII.

CHAPTER XIII.

CHAPTER XIV.

CHAPTER XV.

INTRODUCTION.

The proper adjustment of the National debt, and the establishment of a *National* System of finance, is the great and all-absorbing question to be settled. In fact it is the Aaron's rod of the hour, which, if it does not swallow up all other issues at no distant day, it will be a consuming fire to burn out the industrial interests of the nation. If the question of finance does not become a disturbing element which is destined immediately to agitate this whole country as it has never before been agitated, it is not from any lack of importance, but because its over-shadowing power has not been manifested in such a manner as fully to attract the attention of the public mind. The vague, undefined, and indescribable presentiment of the people, in relation to this incubus power, although they have failed to comprehend it, may be sufficient to arouse inquiry, and to suggest the propriety of considering the matter well, before they permit the nation to take a final plunge into the bottomless ocean of European consols and European finance. Financiers, pleased with the delightful prospect of one hundred and forty-five millions of dollars annual gold interest, as a commencement, may overlook the small item of hard blows which labor must deal to earn this trifling annual tribute paid to capital, before laborers can be permitted to feed and clothe their own families. But insignificant as this small item of labor may appear to the donee, the donor will not fail to weigh the task with different *scales*, and to treasure well the lesson taught.

A consumed or minus capital, which, through interest, gnaws at the vitals of labor, at the rate of twenty-four millions of dollars per year faster than England's hated debt, will not fail to make itself felt in a nation's depleted granaries and empty purses. This amphisbæna of European despots, will crawl in every direction to scent out labor and its products. What can not be secured to capitalists in the form of bonds, can easily be gobbled up in National banking, based on these bonds. In this complicated machinery lies hid the power which determines the price of labor and of property without regard to the cost of production, or the compensation of the laborer. In this, too, lies the unequal annual distribution of property between laborers and the so-called capitalists. As the nation is now, or soon will be, afloat upon these questions and upon the reconstruction of a new system, will it not be well for the people themselves to understand what is included in this reconstruction issue? Reconstruction in its wider meaning, includes not only the establishment of civil order in the South, but the re-arrangement of our industrial and financial system North and South.

This condition of the industrial and financial affairs of the nation, while it is apparently the legitimate fruits of war, is really the fruits of a false system which war has probed down to the bottom and brought out to public view. Heretofore our financial laws have been the outcroppings of monarchy. Notwithstanding our Republican or Democratic theories of government, our monetary laws are merely a reflex, or a very vicious imitation of the English system, an ingenious, artful, overreaching device invented by financiers and statesmen in the interest of kings,—supreme selfishness schooled in kingcraft, and steeped in despotism. Finance, thus originating, may properly be defined to be the genteel kingly art of rendering a very small incidental benefit to the governed, for the purpose, primarily, of securing the more essential rewards of industry to the non-industrial and non-useful governing or controlling class. In ancient and barbarous times, when the power of the king depended upon the length of his spear, or his expertness with *that* and his bow and arrow—a banking bow and arrow finance, an exchequer bill, or the kingly currency was a notched stick, and his royal revenues were gathered and exchanged by it, his exchequer and his granaries were filled by tithing. The real character of this finance or the doctrine of the divine right of kings which is the foundation of the whole system, may be thus vulgarly expressed: the Divine Being through this divine bow and arrow, of mine, has ordained that unto us is committed the labor to govern, and unto *you*, OUR well beloved subjects, is *allotted* the important duty of doing the work. You and yours shall earn the living, and I and mine are ordained to eat it. This is the divine right of royalty. In my sacred person is justice and judgment; I decree what shall be done, and thou shalt do it; kings command but subjects *must* obey. The primary law of obedience is to feed royalty. Its dignity and its power must be maintained at the expense of labor without regard to the interests or the rights of the laborer. Royalty is, therefore, a nightmare enthroned on the back of labor. But the tithing by which royalty was supported, was only adapted to answer the purpose of a very ignorant and barbarous age; an age when a notched stick furnished a circulating medium, and was the king's accountant; an age when the royal signet or seal manual stamped on wax might be a convenient mode of supplying a royal misfortune—the great inconvenience of not being able to write. When a higher intelligence superseded this ignorance and barbarism, the king's exchequer bill changed its form, and his exchequer was filled by a mode more convenient than tithing. So long as his supplies depended materially upon the length of his bow or the swiftness of his arrow, a portion of the annual fruits of industry and the increase of the flocks and herds could be gathered by a royal tithing decree; this answered all the purposes of well fed royalty, and the empty stomach of the subject was a fitting symbol of loyalty.

But in a more advanced stage of society tithing is too expensive, and the king is cheated out of too many pigs, lambs, turkeys, geese and chickens. Besides long transporting lines are suggestive. They might suggest the inconvenience of this ancient revenue procedure, or raise a doubt as to the king's right. Hence, royalty might be contaminated by too near contact with the ignoble many. The sober enquiry of subjects, sharpened by the serious suggestions of an empty stomach might prove very damaging to royalty and loyalty. To avoid unpleasant enquiries, expedite exchanges and furnish the king and his retainers their supplies, required a cheaper, more expeditious and less suggestive system of finance. But it must not be forgotten that in those early ages of the world as well as to-day, the essential requisite of finance was to benefit the ruling class—to enable the subject or citizen to make an easy and just exchange of his products is the merest incident. Hence, the representative power of money—its accumulation by way of interest—its control thereby over property, and its exchanges, impost duties, licenses, stamp-acts, and other similar ingenious, but delusive devices, which are necessary to support royalty without enquiry and at the expense of labor, are the substance of the ancient royal tithe. If tithing was oppressive, how has the modern financial devices improved the matter ? Let Europe's pauperized and nobility-ridden laborers answer. From these prolific sources of kingcraft, selfishness, public weal and inexorable necessity, the doctrine of representatives or bonds and money were born.

When political economists, therefore, attempt to trace the medium of exchange back to the division of labor as its source, and thus to account for this labor robbing system of money, or when they claim the system as the result of an honest effort of human wisdom, and the insurmountable difficulties which legislators have experienced in their attempt to found a just system, it is simply the play of Hamlet, with Hamlet left out. It is a kingdom without a king. If not a headless system, it is a body with a false head. The motive or governing power is hid beneath the rubbish of specious terms, it makes labor and its necessities the creating or forming power. The central principle or the divine right of kings under this fine spun theory is merely the passive agent, which, under the genius and all controlling sway of a diversified industry, has brought into the world this representative monstrosity of labor called money. This is a libel upon labor. Industry is the handmaid of honesty. She blesses the world with fruitful fields, provides our habitations, feeds and clothes us, and furnishes us with the useful and ornamental things of life. But she has seldom tried her well trained and skillful hand in the magic art of forming governmental systems, or for securing her own rights. If these results are to be attained; if the world is to have a financial system, the product of labor, and therefore its honest and efficient agent, it must be the work of the coming age, and labor must gird herself with strength to fill the long delayed requirement. The labor element of the world has been the pack-horse of kingly policies and kingly power without compensation long enough, and it is for the American people now to cut loose from European policies and this European finance, to build an American system based upon the property and sovereignty of the people and the inviolability of their rights. Why should we continue to pattern after their false systems, unless it is for the re-production of Europe here?

Our governmental theory recognizes the people not as subjects but as sovereigns. Why should not our laws conform to our Government theory? If the people are competent to choose their rulers, why are they not competent to choose their money? If they are competent to furnish all the products, why are they not competent to furnish the money to exchange their products? If money is made solely for the purpose of exchanging products, why should it not be under the control of those who have products to exchange? If the people, through the Government, have the exclusive power to coin money and regulate its value, why should not the money be under the exclusive and direct control of the power which creates it? If the people, through the Government, have the power to say what shall be money, and how much shall be had, why permit any body else to interfere in this matter? If Government bonds are to be the base of the money, why not give the bonds for the money and the money for the bonds? If the government or the people are good as surety why not as principal? If the people who earn the property do not know how much money they need to exchange that property how can the bankers tell them? Why should government and people be under the perpetual pupilage of soulless corporations, heartless money-changers and gambling stock jobbers? If the capitalists have furnished the money and taken the government bond is not the bond and the interest full pay for the money? If so, why should they be permitted to have back their money and draw interest on their money and on the bond? Is not one interest enough? If the farmer furnished the grain and has taken a bond why not let him have back his grain with the privilege of drawing interest on that and on his bond? So of the soldier and every man who has furnished the government material aid. Again, if the bondholder furnished money to the government worth forty cents on the dollar at the time of furnishing it, if he is to have the sixty per cent. paid to him by now agreeing to pay him in gold? Why not pay the soldier and the farmer and every body else in the same manner and at the same rate ? But, above all, what will be the effect of destroying the greenback and surrendering up to the capitalists the exclusive right to furnish the money? Will they not thereby be enabled to draw a double interest out of labor to control the price of labor, products, and government bonds ? If the government desires to pay the bonds or lower the rates of interest, must it not do so upon the capitalist's own terms—the sale of bonds at a large discount, or by an increased taxation of the people ? These are the serious questions presented not merely for congress to settle, but the working men and business classes; they must decide, and that, too, promptly. The *interest* of capitalists will now be pressed upon congress with all the force which money and talent can command. Their pensioned attorneys will occupy not only the lobbies but representative and senate halls. Where are the people's advocates and what are they doing ? Will they tamely submit to be thus badgered and cozzened in the destruction of the greenback and in the payment of the bond in gold ? These questions are too serious to be trifled with and too urgent to admit a moment's delay. If the people desire their rights they must look after them at once, and determine for themselves what legislation their interests demand. If a farmer seeks a farm or a business man the choice of a business for life, personal attention is needed. How much more important is the question which is to determine the distribution of the property of a great nation, giving to each an opportunity to obtain his just share of the annual products instead of dividing them between the producer and capitalists by law, and thus binding heavy burdens on the shoulders of the former solely for the benefit of the latter. And let it not be overlooked—the instrumentality by which all that is effected is national bonds and the national institution of money. We must now either adopt a new system and one which respects the rights of the people or else we must continue the old—the present fluctuating, labor-robbing and business-destroying financiers system. To determine these questions intelligently requires an accurate knowledge of the character and effect of fundamental laws, and especially those relating to national bonds and the institution of money.

CHAPTER I.

ABSTRACT OR IDEAL MONEY.

BYRON in his Don Juan commences by saying: "I want a hero, not an uncommon want." This certainly is not our want. We are surfeited with heroes and would-be heroes. The serious question, however, with us is: How shall we get down to the affairs of every day life, and not break our necks in the descent? We have upturned every thing. Upon us the ends of the world have fallen. Our conglomerate fabric of Democratic or Republican theories, based upon the European *heirloom* of feudalism, has met a sad fate. It is useless now to spend time in quarreling over what might have been. What *was* has been wiped out in fields of blood. What is to be is a question and a work for the future to solve. We cannot revivify the dead carcass of the dead past. Let the dead therefore bury its dead, and let the American people resolutely set themselves to work to upbuild an American system, which, as a whole, shall respect their rights. It is the *people* who have to pay for the governmental administration of justice, whether good or ill—their *property* and their *lives* must answer for all the crude, selfish, false theories and misdeeds of rulers.

The barbaric origin of money and the changes which an advancing civilization has brought has been alluded to in the preceding pages. The special province of this chapter will be to unfold the philosophy and use of ideal moneys—or the moneys of account used in every civilized nation. Without a knowledge of this branch of the subject it is difficult, if not impossible, to unfold the science of money. Gold and silver are commodities of great value. Though by no means as useful as many other metals, yet for thousands of years they have maintained their ascendancy as an universal equivalent for all balances in the commercial world. The extravagant estimate placed upon them smacks so strongly of the doctrine of the divine right of kings, that it is impossible to resist the inference that both have a common origin. These metals, however, as coin, are simply legal standards of payment, arbitrarily determined by statute law.

How far they are thus used as a medium of exchange, what necessity exists for such use, and precisely what that use is, the people have a right to know. For possibly it may be true that the office or use of coin is not exactly what it is generally imagined to be. A better knowledge of the subject may disclose the fact that many of the supposed functions of coin are purely imaginary; that these functions, even if they exist, can be better performed through other less expensive agencies. Among these agencies which require to be examined, and more thoroughly understood, is the subject of *ideal money*, or the *money of account.*

By ideal money, or money of account, is meant a denominational or money unit and its fractional or decimal parts, as for instance, dollars and cents, pounds, shillings and pence, etc. It is a *numeral* of value or the language of prices in which commercial dealings are carried on, contracts made, prices expressed, and books of account kept. Or, in other words, it is the mental image of value which the constant use of these denominational *units* with their fractional or decimal parts, thus creates and fixes in the mind. It is a mental habit pertaining to civilization in use in all ages of the world.

Its origin may have been from an actual comparison of, and by a perfect familiarity with, some material article of intrinsic worth, as a coin or a metal of a certain quality of fineness and weight; but, however it may have originated anciently is a question of little practical importance at the present time.

At this age of the world, men do not gain a knowledge of values nor learn to estimate them by comparing one thing with another, any more than they gain a knowledge of arithmetical numbers, and of their powers, by comparing them with fingers— but they do gain a knowledge of these denominational money units, in the same manner that they gain a knowledge of arithmetical numbers—and their power, as applied to values in fixing prices and estimating values is similar to that of numbers in ascertaining and determining quantities. People in the constant practice of naming prices, making contracts, debiting, crediting and settling accounts, thus acquire a knowledge and judgment of prices and values which forms in the mind an ideal or mental scale of equal parts which enables its practised possessor instantly, and almost without effort, to understand the market price or value of all articles, commodities, or services, and by arithmetical numbers, without any additional aid from either coin or bullion, to be able to determine with the utmost accuracy their actual value and amount.

Sir James Stewart thus defines an ideal money, or the money of account, and describes its uses:

"Money, which I call of account, is no more than a scale of equal parts, invented for measuring the respective value of things vendible.

"Money of account is, therefore, quite a different thing from money coin, and might exist although there was no such thing in the world as any substance which could become an adequate and proportional equivalent for every commodity.

"Money of account performs the same office, with regard to the value of things that degrees, minutes, seconds, etc., do with regard to angles, or as scales do to geographical maps, or to plans of any kind.

"In all these inventions there is some denominative taken for the unit.

In angles, it is the degree; in geography, it is the mile; in plans, foot and yard; in money, it is the pound, livre, florin, etc.

"The degree has no determinate length, so neither has that part of the scale, upon plans or maps which marks the unit; the usefulness of all these being solely confined to the marking of proportions.

"Just so, the unit in money can have no invariable determinate proportion to any part of value; that is to say, it cannot be fixed in perpetuity to any particular quantity of gold and silver, or any other commodity.

"The value of commodities depending upon circumstances relative to themselves, their value ought to be considered as changing with respect to one another only; consequently, any thing which troubles or perplexes the ascertaining these changes of proportion by the means of a general determinate and invariable scale, must be hurtful to trade; and this is the infalliable consequence of every rise in the price of money or coin.

"Money, as has been said, is an ideal scale of equal parts. If it be demanded, what ought to be the standard value of one part, I answer by putting another question: What is the standard length of a degree, a minute, or a second? None; and there is no necessity of any other than what, by convention, mankind think fit to give.

"The first step being perfectly arbitrary, people may adjust one or more of these parts to a precise quantity of the precious metals; and so soon as this is done, and that money becomes realized, as it were in gold and silver, then it acquires a new definition; it then becomes the price as well as the measure of value.

"It does not follow from this adjusting of the metal to the scale of value, that they themselves should become the scale."

A florin banco has a more determinate value than a pound of fine gold or silver; this bank money stands invariable like a rock in the sea.—Sir James Stewart's Political Economy, B. 3, chap. 1, Vol. I, 4th Ed. p. 226.

The distinction then between the term money as denoting prices, in keeping books of account, in making promissory notes, bills of exchange, national bonds, currency, and all instruments denoting commercial value as used in carrying on business; and the *term* money, as applied to coin or legal tender money, used in making payment, is a radical one, and is the key for unlocking some of the most difficult problems which financial science presents.

It is easy to run the eye over a journal and note at a glance several hundred entries of sums debited for goods sold, varying from ten to five hundred dollars, and by the use of this mental language, or ideal money, thus fixed in the mind, in a few moments to determine accurately the whole sum.

If, however, the exact amount of coin denoted by the several entries thus made were placed before the accountant, he might not be able to determine accurately the several denominations of coin and their value, and if he could, it might take the accountant hours, and even weeks, to examine and count the coin.

Coins may be changed every month, and even every week, but so long as they do not infringe upon or change this ideal money or money of account, no serious derangement in the method of estimating prices or values would occur. But the least change in the denominational value of this money unit, *numeral* or ideal language of prices, will take half a century, at least, to accustom the people to such an alteration in their mental modes of estimating values. These facts are well illustrated in the colonial moneys of account of the United States and Canada. There never was a coin out of which these moneys of account originated. In the more retired portions of the United States there are now, or there were a few years since, many persons to be found who continue to use these colonial moneys of account of pounds, shillings and pence, as they were wont to do in colonial times before separation from Great Britain.

The *term* or unit pound in the several Colonies named, are given in the following table as expressed in our present money of account—that it may be seen what changes may be made, in the modes of estimating, through the agency of a deranged money of account, and what will be the effect of such changes on the people's interest, will be more fully shown when we come to treat upon that subject or the causes which produce a deranged money of account:—

£1. New England and Virginia, is equal to	$333 or 6s. to the Dollar.	
" New York and North Carolina, to	250 or 8s	" "
" Pennsylvania and Middle States,	266 or 7s. 6d.	"
" South Carolina,	427 or 4s. 8d.	"

The French inhabitants of Lower Canada furnish a remarkable instance of the tenacity with which people cling to their moneys of account. These French Canadians continue to express their prices and make all their estimates of coin, and all other values, in their old money of account by livres, sous and deniers, although the coin from whence the mental idea originated has passed out of use in that portion of the country for nearly a century. These people, too, are surrounded by a population and are under laws and customs where another money of account of an entirely different character is in use. The Canadians of English descent also use a money of account—ideal or mental money, although it is in pounds, shillings and pence, differing materially from that of the mother country. The following table will exhibit the manner in which the various coins are estimated in the moneys of account in the British provinces of North America:

Coins.	Nova Scotia Halifax.			Lower Canada.			Upper Canada.			Prince Edward's Island.		
	£.	s.	d.	£.	s.	d.	£.	s.	d.	£.	s.	d.
British Guinea,	1	3	4	1	3	5	1	5	6	—	—	—
" Sovereign,	1	5	0	—	—	—	1	4	4	1	10	0
American Eagle,	2	10	0	—	—	—	—	—	—	3	2	6
British Crown,	—	—	—	0	5	6	0	6	0	0	7	6
" Shilling,	—	—	—	0	1	1	0	1	3	0	1	6
American Dollar,	0	5	0	0	5	0	0	6	0	0	6	3
French Crown,	0	5	5	0	5	6	—	—	—	—	—	—
" Five Franck,	0	4	7	0	4	8	—	—	—	—	—	—

Martine's British Colonies, page 229, and appendix 53, Colwell, page 57.

In the British Islands the units of the moneys of account are as follows :—

Jamaica, £1 sterling equals	£1 8s.	or 7s. to the Dollar.
Barbadoes, " "	1 7	or 6s. " "
Windward Islands, "	1 15	or 8s. " "
Leeward Islands, "	2 0	or 9s. " "

Facts of this character might be multiplied indefinitely from the history of every age and nation, but these alone are amply sufficient to *show* that men do not measure values in a civilized state of society, whatever may have been their practice in barbarous times by means of gold and silver coins, or by their substitutes of paper money or bank notes, but their estimates are made by the ideal or mental image fixed in the mind by constant use of the language of prices. The same mental habit is manifest in the use of figures, numerals, or the denominations of weights, measures in distances, and in time. This mental habit and its uses may be tested by the attempt to form an idea of space or weight, quantity, time, or value in gross, without the aid of these arbitrary, mental subdivisions. Or it may be better illustrated, perhaps, by attempting to form an idea of values in the money of account of a nation, other than that in which a person has been educated. For instance, let an American attempt to estimate the value of a large number of separate parcels of goods, lands, grain or other property, in large amounts, in the money of account of Great Britain or France—or to increase and complicate the matter still more, let him attempt to make the estimate of value and quantity—the value in pounds, shillings, and pence, and the quantity of grain, together with its price, under the cental system, by hundreds of pounds, and their fractional or decimal parts of a hundred, instead of by dollars, and by bushels. When this experiment has been fully tried and solved it will give some idea of the value and use of ideal or mental moneys and measurments as fixed in the mind by the use of these various denominational units of value, by every day estimate of value, weights, distances, etc.

If, however, these facts do not furnish convincing proofs that it is by this mental or ideal money that estimates of value are made, or if it is claimed that it is the coin or metal which furnishes the measurement, or accurate estimate, and not the mental idea, how will these materialistic reasoners account for the fact of values being estimated for centuries in the moneys of account in the case of the bank moneys of Venice, Genoa, Amsterdam, etc.—as is shown in the chapters where these banks are treated of—or how will they otherwise account for the estimates of value in pounds, shillings, and pence. In the case of children born in England, and who became men, during the specie suspension—this was declared by act of parliament in 1798, though it actually existed a long period anterior to that date, and was continued up to the year 1822—or to take our own history, or that of the other colonies of Great Britain, some periods of which no coin or bank paper was in general use for a long number of years, and no coin of the denominations there used ever existed. The earliest periods of time which this writer can bring to his recollection are intimately connected with estimating values by the Pennsylvania colonial money of account and without having any coin of that denomination, 7s. 6d. to the dollar. Values, too, were estimated in bulk or by quantity, as the giving so many days' labor for a certain article or other service. Two and a half bushels of wheat was the price of making a woolen cloth coat. Two and a half bushels of wheat became the measure of making a coat. The mode of estimating values by the colonial money of account has not been entirely eradicated after long years of practice in estimating in the money of account formed by the use of dollars and cents. This illustrates the early use of metals in first forming the mental habit. The present suspension of specie payments will very probably produce a state of financial affairs which will last so long that the generation which is now coming on to the stage will have no knowledge of estimating values by any pretended use of coin. Will it be claimed that the idea of value which these instances furnish, receive any material aid from the legal *standard* coins or that the estimate of value formed by persons under the influences named, will be any less accurate, or less reliable, than the ideas of value obtained through the constant and actual use of coin. It is affirmed, then, that the use of coin will make no difference whatever; that if no coin should ever again be issued from the mint, people of every nation, unless some disturbing cause intervenes, would continue perpetually to estimate values in the money of account in which they were educated the same as they do to-day.

In a treatise, therefore, on money, to leave out ideal money, or the money of account, is like leaving out the voice in conversation, or in vocal music, or of arithmetic, in treating of mathematics. This ideal money is the very language of finance. It is as much the *numeral* of value as figures are of amounts.— It is in fact the written and unwritten language and law of values and prices expressed in all contracts, agreements, or instruments or securities, used in commerce or business for the exchange of commodities or compensation for services—and thus becomes an essential part of the mental constitution of the man himself. The want of attention to the real agency of this ideal money leads to indefinite ideas of the uses and power of money. How frequently we hear it asserted that coin is the standard measure of values the world over. Yet, if a standard, how is it used? The fact is, that these coins have to be adjusted accurately to moneys of account of every nation. Every division and sub-division must respect and be nicely adjusted to these mental habits of the people for whose use they are intended. Unless these are respected it would be almost impossible to do business. Persons speak of the "power of money," when the power of credit is meant. A merchant inquires the price of five hundred chests of tea, the price is named in the money of account to which he is accustomed; he makes the purchase and gives his note for the amount; money exercised no power, or any other influence in the transaction. It was not the "power of money," but of credit. The money of account enabled the parties to understand each other, and complete the bargain. It is the power of credit, based upon commercial integrity, which transfers and re-transfers nine-tenths of the property of the country. Neither coin nor paper money made a legal tender, are standards of value, measures of value, nor are they representatives of value—but they are merely arbitrary and legal standards of payment. As for coins, they are seldom used, and much the greater share of payments is made in currency which is not a legal tender, and, therefore, is not money.

When it is asserted that money is a standard of value, a measure of value, and a representative of value, what is meant? How can a mere arbitrary enactment, providing that a certain article or commodity of intrinsic value, or, one possessing no intrinsic value, but given certain legal properties, or qualities, to render it an end of the law, by way of payment, be either a standard of value, measure of value, or a representative of value? The origin of value is labor, intrinsic qualities, and usefulness—the cost of production by labor. The intrinsic qualities, which adapt it for a limited, or a more extensive use, and the extent of the demand, with the scantiness or fulness of supply, these are the real ingredients which go to make up value. Use therefore, may correctly be said to be the only substantial measure of value, and price in the language of the money of account, or the ideal or mental division of value, as by dollars, pounds, shillings, is the mode of expressing or estimating this value. The necessity, therefore, of having this denominational unit or ideal money with its several decimal or fractional parts definitely expressed, and well understood, is all-important. It is really a denominational subdivision of the value in a commodity, or of service, into equal and• distinct parts—for the more easy comprehension of the amount, and for the greater facility in estimating it. All the measurement of values which is ever made, is the application of this denominational scale in the naming of prices, and estimating the value. No coin or other legal money is employed to express the price, or to indicate what the purchaser or seller would give or take. A coin dollar is made a legal equivalent for a denominational dollar's worth of wheat; the wheat dollar being determined by the market, and the gold dollar after having at some period been determined to be a dollar by the market also, the law seizes upon that point of the market, arbitrarily determines that the gold whether it is worth it or not, shall remain a dollar, and a legal equivalent for a market value dollar. It has no application in the determination of the value of the wheat or any other commodity. If it measured the wheat, it would have to be produced and applied to the measurement. If one man should desire to have a yard of cloth measured, he would on this principle go to the merchant, and take his cloth, and the merchant would give him his yard stick. The gold dollar being arbitrarily fixed by law, and the wheat dollar by the natural law of supply and demand, both values are designated by the term dollar in the money of account. When a man says to another, that horse is worth a hundred dollars, he means that the horse value divided up into a hundred value parts is correctly expressed by the term one hundred dollars—horse dollars. If these horse dollars had been expressed in colonial pounds, shillings, and pence, it would be equally horse pounds, shillings and pence, but as there never was a coin of these denominations, it can be easily seen that no coin was the horse measure, and it is equally so in every other case. Coins are therefore, in no correct sense measures of value, and they are not so used.

The same train of reasoning applies to the doctrine of representatives. Coins are neither a sign nor a representative of value—they represent no properties of value, but such as are contained in them as metals ; they represent no properties of value in anything else but gold, and in the uses to which they are naturally applicable. Legal enactments cannot change these properties, and make them what they are not, and cannot be. By making them a legal equivalent in payment, does not in any correct sense make them represent the articles paid for by them. They are a legal substitute, but nothing more. That is all the use they are made to perform in making an exchange. They do not, and cannot perform the functions, nor represent them, as contained in the articles for which they are exchanged. This loose use of language may be justly attributed, either to not understanding the functions of a money of account, or else to paying no attention to the denominational way values are expressed.

The term, standard of value, is equally objectionable. Any article which possesses a certain amount of valuable qualities, applicable to any particular use, and to an amount, which by its use is denominated a dollar, is a common equivalent for any other article which has qualities to the amount of one dollar, this value to be determined in the same manner by the use to which it is applicable, as in the first mentioned case. There is no such thing as a common standard of value, to which all articles can be referred, and by which they can be truly said to be measured. When nations, therefore, make either gold or silver, or any other commodity, a legal equivalent in payment of certain specified amounts of value, it is only a legal equivalent for the amount of value thus named. But the word, standard of value, is an ill-chosen term, and as used does not convey a true idea of the office, and the only use, which coin is made to perform by such a law, which is simply a legal equivalent in payment—nothing more, nothing less.

If it is necessary that quantities and qualities of commodities should be accurately ascertained and understood, to make a just exchange, how much more necessary is it, that the index of value should be unerring and invariably just, and then when this is established, that the office or use performed by such agency, and its boundaries, should be accurately ascertained, and understood by the people?

Any influence, therefore, which destroys the integrity of the language of prices or the numeral of value, will breed endless confusion in every branch of business, and gross fraud and injustice cannot be otherwise than the result.

By the intervention of money and currency, the want of value in the medium, and the barter character of exchange has been so far lost sight of, in the medium through which it is effected, that at length it has come to pass that money is considered as the real wealth, which is most to be desired, and the commodity is a drug or thing of little value, which must go begging to find somebody who will be kind enough to give something for it, that it may not be wasted in the hands of the manufacturer, or producer. This confusion of ideas respecting money, and respecting ideal moneys, or the manner in which the estimates of value are actually made, has been cultivated and nursed: first, by coinage, second, by bank paper, pretended to be based on coins, or secured by a small portion of coins, mortgages, state or national bonds, or some other deceptive device. Here is furnished an actual value in the coin as a commodity, but not as a coin or money, and an apparent value in the securities. Thus, the money power, or the legal power, which made it money, is lost sight of, in the ostentatious display of coin and securities, upon which the money was supposed to be based. Although, little of these securities or guaranties, are, or were of use to the public, when it becomes necessary to test the value. To make the money good, it must be rightly instituted, not liable to change. The people too, must understand this, that they may have confidence in it, and they must also have clear views of each and every process or agency employed, or used, in making exchange, and the importance and value of each.

If it is supposed, that money is only good, by the commodity value it possesses, and not by its legal attributes, then money, must ever remain simply a commodity, and all exchanges barter, which is the very difficulty, which civilization has been supposed to remove.

Again, if it be imagined, that the mode of estimating values, is by certain definite quantities, and qualities of metal, stamped in a certain definite form by the state—then the actual mode of making estimates, by a money of account, or ideal money, will be lost sight of, and the accurate ascertainment of values will be almost impossible. If the value of all material substances largely change by use, and if this change is frequently in inverse directions, one article going up and the other down, how is certainty to be attained, and of what use are pretended measures thus instituted?

If, on the other hand, men estimate by the mental or ideal money, it is necessary that there should be a point, zero or nought, in the quality of the measure, or, which if it does not express nought, it must not be liable to fluctuation, or change.

If it be true, as is here affirmed, that the sums written in books of account, promissory notes, bills of exchange, National and State bounds, money, currency, etc., in every day use, are not indebted for their present definite meaning to coin or coinage. Then the process through which this result is reached, and the causes if any, which would operate to change the relative value of the *numeral* of this money of account thus used, are important to be understood.

Now, it is a fact not to be denied, that for centuries before our adoption of the dollar unit—as the unit of our money of account, prices were expressed, books kept, and notes given, in pounds, shillings, and pence, without there being any corresponding coin to denote this denominational unit. These denominations were used in the same manner that the dollar unit, or money of account, is used at present. These terms had one significance, as has been shown, in Massachusetts, another in Pennsylvania and the middle States, New York and North Carolina. The value, or power of the unit, differed in each of these States, but was perfectly understood in each, without corresponding units, expressed in coins. It is no more difficult to carry in the mind a unit of value, than an idea of a foot, a yard, a rod, mile, acre, or a pound, ounce, or penny-weight.

Men attain a knowledge of prices, and state them, from the constant use of these denominations, the same as they use numbers. It is not a mechanical, but an arithmetical process, by which a unit taking its name from some legislative act, coin, or some definite weight of gold, or silver, or some other denominational term—is fixed in the mind by daily use—is added, subtracted, multiplied or divided, with the aid of arithmetical numbers.

The precious metals were first used, or given, in exchange for other commodities, at a price agreed upon by the parties, at the time of making the exchange. In time, a general price is put upon all commodities, and by the aid of arithmethic, and the prices thus fixed, sales are made. The price of gold and silver then becomes as well, if not better known, than the price or value of most other articles ; these prices are no longer subject to be fixed by the whim, or caprice of the holder, or the purchaser; they are fixed by general consent, and this makes a market or merchantable value. Governments in fixing the price of metals, by coinage, hide this important fact from the public view. The mint price is intended to be the average market price, at some period. Thus the mint appears to settle the prices, when it only follows in the wake of the market—but this price once thus authoritatively settled, by the mint, ceases to be a matter of public inquiry, until war, or some such disturbing element, so far unsettles the mint adjustment, of the money quality, that gold and silver, as commodities, overleaping all bounds, and all restraints, their values are only known by the increased demand, in the shape of premiums, declared, made in the market from day to day. It then becomes manifest, that the price of gold and silver, like all other articles, fluctuate in the market, simply by the law of supply and demand. Not only so, but when the state fixes her requirement to be paid in coin, not by commodities sold, but by the sale of bonds, upon which not fifty per cent. of their face is realized, she thus increases the demand, by the very law itself, three or four-fold beyond the power of supply, the prices of the metals, for this use, which have generally been so uniform, fluctuate much worse than all other commodities. While the gold gamblers, and stock jobbers, by having control of the circulating medium, are enabled to reap a rich reward by the depreciation of their own currency, after it gets out of their hands. On the other hand they are enabled, by the same means, through governmental aid to concentrate the precious metals, as they are called, and reap a still greater harvest out of the metals by the derangement made. When they have sold out their articles to the government, and people, and taken bonds, bearing large and bankrupting interest, and at these enormously depreciated prices, then the people are told, the currency and the bonds thus depreciated are inflated, that it is necessary to go back to a gold base, in order to cure this inflation—and to be able again to use gold and silver as standards of value—that people cannot estimate values by anything else, but that gold and silver, with the large premiums, are merely commodities. Gold and silver are at all times simply commodities, subject like other commodities to the market price, and coinage and currency laws only obscure or hide not only this fact from the people, but it also hides the gross outrages perpetrated by this double shield of villany constructed by law.

This complicated machinery is well understood by dealers in coin, and bullion brokers, and intelligent merchants; they very well know that the mint price is intended to be the market price of the gold; they are also well aware, however, that it is the mint regulations, which upholds the steady price of gold and silver, throughout the world; that the moment these gold laws are removed, these metals will seek a natural level of value very different from present rates, and very possibly an innovation of just laws in place of monopolizing and unjust ones, might occasion the loss of their control over gold and the markets. But, while these facts are well known to the classes above named, very few of the business community, or of the people understand this, nor do they think or know, that they are almost entirely indebted to the money of account, and not to coins, for the facility with which they estimate their values, and make all their varied computations.

The derangement of prices and values, which they so much deplore, are from these coinage and gold bond laws, which they are taught, are instituted to protect their rights. But for these unjust laws, markets would uniformly be governed by the law of supply and demand, and their money of account would always be a true index of prices and values.

This mental proclivity, thus manifested in these moneys of account, throughout the world, is a commercial necessity. It would be next to impossible in the present diversified state of coinage to carry on business, and to express by the number of coins, which would be an equivalent for the price, and amount of business now being done.

The same effort, which is necessary to enable persons to remember the coin and its value is sufficient to enable them, to carry the memory of that denominational value in the mind, and to use it with the same effect abstractly or mentally, as if referring to the coin itself. It is thus, therefore, that every coin, or certain weight of gold or silver, or other denomination, or term of value used for any considerable period of time, becomes the money of account. This abstract measure, or unit of value, is used arithmetically to express and estimate all values. It is thus made as capable of expressing changes, in the value of these metals, as that of any other commodity When this money of account has become once established in the mind, it has a fixed value—it is a permanent mental possession not easily eradicated. This index of value, too, remains permanent and unchangeable, independent of the fluctuations and changes of the article from which it took its rise. A person who is accustomed only to the use of these denominational terms, estimates values without any knowledge derived from the use of coins, as readily, and accurately, as those who have used coins.

This distinction, however, between the money of account, or between the mental idea and the money itself, is not apprehended by all persons with equal facility. Indeed, it is a subject, which requires earnest attention and accurate discrimination fully to comprehend it. Moliere, says Colwell, introduces a character in one of his comedies, seeking an education suitable for a gentleman advanced in years, who found to his great surprise as well as pleasure, that without a master all his life time he had been speaking prose.

Thus, men use mental or abstract moneys to estimate values a whole life time, without being so much as aware of what they have been doing.

This mental-money-idea is so fastened in the mind by making estimates, hourly and daily, that it becomes such a part and parcel of the mind, that men cannot estimate or comprehend values otherwise.

The people of Great Britain, France and United States, though flooded with the coinage of the world, would without any coins continue to estimate values, for the next hundred years, in the language of their moneys of account.

It is not the gold sovereign, pounds, shillings, and pence, in England, nor is it the coin dollar, dimes and cents, in the United States, but it is the scale of equal parts fixed in the mind by the use of these various terms, which enables the inhabitants of the several countries to estimate values so readily. If these coins rise in the market in England, it would be quoted as £1, 3s. 8d., etc., in the United States at $1.05—10—15, as the market premium might be ; yet the standard coin, in payment, is £1, $1.00.

When the pound sterling is used in the United States, it is estimated in dollars and cents by our money of account—and the eagle in England in the same manner, in pounds, shillings and pence.

The transactions in business of every country are carried on by books of account, notes, bonds, and other instruments in writing and printing, computations are made and all the conversation respecting prices and values, is in this financial or ideal language of the money of account, whereas coins are seldom used or referred to in ordinary business.

It is not strange then that men should use this language, or the language of their every day business, and make all their computations and estimates of value by it. It would be strange were it otherwise.

If the philosophy of this mode of estimating values has not been as well understood and appreciated as it ought to have been, yet the fact that men do thus estimate, is well known to every thorough business man, accountant and cambist.

But while this language occupies so prominent a place in the experimental knowledge of the capitalists, merchant and banker. Statesmen, political economists, and theoretical writers, seem to be so absorbed in the commodity or barter properties of coin, that they wholly ignore the essential and indispensible uses of a money of account, and the chasm of hundreds of years between civilization and barbarism, is thus continually being bridged over by legal enactments and financial treatises, which teach mankind that they must not only measure values by chunks of gold, but they must keep, and transport them thousands of miles to be used as a medium, to make a valid exchange of a horse for an ass.

In state papers, and in the discussions of financial questions in legislative assemblies, it is not an unusual occurrence to find these high functionaries so frequently confounding the obvious distinctions between the offices or uses of coin, and those of a money of account—as to raise a suspicion that this subject is not well understood, or else they are entirely indifferent as to the ideas which language should convey.

Colwell in a note gives a notable instance of the kind from the writings of Leon Faucher, who says: "The effective money in the middle ages varying constantly, and being at the mercy of every prince to be altered at his will, they devised a money of account, a sort of abstract or fictitious unit, which might remain relatively invariable, in the midst of monetary fluctuations, caused by the unskilfulness or the bad faith of governments, and the custom is preserved in some states, to-day." *Sur l'or et sur l'argent*, page 5.

This is the view of ideal moneys entertained by a minister of finance, in France. A man of ability, who knew full well, or ought to have known the essential use which is rendered in business through this instrumentality in every age of the world. This eminent man was in fact using it every hour in the day;

could not transact business without it, and yet he ascribes its use as belonging to the middle ages.

But Monsieur Faucher is not the only man who has made this or similar mistakes by not fully apprehending the manner in which men estimate values. An examination of Presidential messages, secretaries and finance committees' reports, of Senate and House, would, it is to be feared, show, that they not only misapprehended the functions of a money of account, but very possibly it might disclose a most appalling want of knowledge upon the subject of money itself. If this knowledge is prevalent in legislative circles, it is not very clearly perceived, how that fact is manifest, when coinage is held to be a standard of value, or why it is imagined, that a return to specie payments can compensate, or remove the losses occasioned by the destruction of property in a four years gigantic war, and the removal of more than two millions of men from their ordinary occupations of useful industry during that long period of time. Much less is it understood how the changing of the value of paper, which marks the increased cost of production, can be improved by reducing the circulation much below the actual wants of business.

Men must live, and property must be exchanged, whether we have gold and silver, or not, and the money of account, will, if let alone, accurately mark the increased cost of production, and do no injustice to the people.

When a merchant says a yard of cloth is worth a dollar, the price and quantity of cloth are instantly known, without either coin or yard stick. If the payment is made in coin, and that agrees in name with the denomination used, that seems to prove the idea that the price was measured by the coin; but, if the payment is made in a different denomination of value, as in pounds, shillings, and pence, then it clearly would be otherwise.

Salesmen are frequently employed in making sales, in naming prices and estimating values, in large amounts, who can neither estimate these values in bullion, by weight, nor in foreign coin.

Whoever examines the subject with care, will find that sales of large amounts are seldom paid in coin, and when so made, the coin and bullion, have to be estimated as well as other commodities in the money of account. To call these coins standards of value, is not only a great error, but one, which ought everywhere to be condemned as destroying all correct ideas of the mode of estimating values.

The unit of the moneys of account in France, England, and the United States, agrees with their coins and its functions, are as well performed here as elsewhere, yet attaching the money of account, to a coin of changeable value, and thus giving it a fixed value, by the law of legal tender, is of very questionable utility, to say the least of it. As the value of the money unit if the coin falls in value, and continues there for any considerable period of time, will fall with the coin. England has really four moneys of account—the pound is one unit—the shilling, penny and farthing, are the others. It has been proposed to change the three latter, and have them absorbed in the former. But English statesmen very well understand that the difficulty in the way of the proposed change, is not a question of coinage, but one arising out of the mental habits of the people. Change the unit value of the shilling by law, and the people will continue to reckon in shillings, for the next half century.

The principal money of account now used in the United States is the dollar unit, and its decimals of dimes, etc. It is generally expressed as $1\frac{10}{100}$ instead of ten cents. Before the Revolution there were as has already been shown, several different moneys of account in use, in the different colonies, originating from various causes, such as unfavorable exchange, but no mint or coins established these several units.

The lowering of the value of the unit, used in different countries, originated from very different causes. In England, France, and the other European nations, abusive and fraudulent changes in the coinage, caused the value of the units of these several moneys of account to fall. Whilst in the colonies, which now constitute the United States, the first settlers brought their money of account with them from England. In process of time, over-importation continued unfavorable exchanges, bad crops, and a worthless paper currency, caused the unit of value to fall, varying essentially in different colonies. Pennsylvania had much the best currency—it was in fact a government money, so valuable that other colonies used it for purposes of making exchange.

When the heavy balances against the colonies were finally adjusted, it left their moneys of account, where the depreciated currencies had carried them.

The Spanish dollar formed a common unit, into which all the various moneys of account in use in the different colonies, could be readily translated, so as to enable the people to deal with each other. There can be no pretense that these ideal moneys took their rise from any coin, for none such ever existed. But the Spanish dollar probably furnished the unit, for the money of account of New York and N. Carolina, as it afterwards prepared the way for the adoption of the decimal system of the United States, through a general money of account, formed from its use, and confirmed and made perpetual by subsequent legislative enactment.

The injuries arising from a deranged money of account are incalculable. The loss occasioned by lowering the value of the coin, or changing the unit value of a money of account, deranges all the business of a nation. In the case of coin, the principal fraud is not in the debased coin itself, but in its application to express the value of other property; in this particular the same effect follows from a deranged money of account. The denominational unit representing one amount, and that a lesser one than is supposed, to that extent the people are defrauded. Even when understood, it is difficult to adjust prices to the new scale. Few men have any conception of the injury, which will be inflicted in the business of a whole nation, by misapprehending the value of the unit to the amount of one per cent. If the annual production of property, in the United States, is $1,500,000,000, the use of a money unit deranged one per cent., will occasion a loss of $15,000,000, in one exchange, and if the aggregate of the exchanges should amount to one exchange per week in one year, it would have occasioned a loss of seven hundred and eighty millions of dollars.

If there is a coin of the same denomination of the unit of the moneys of account, for instance, gold or silver dollars, and a depreciation of the coin should take place to the amount of twenty per cent, a gradual accomodation of the money of account, if this depreciation should continue for a great length of time, is sure to follow the downward value of the coin. This depreciation of the coin, and the consequent derangement of the money unit, will first be manifested in the great commercial marts of the world, by the decreased demand for coin; this change is sooner discovered by dealers in bullion and coin, and, therefore, they are enabled by their superior knowledge to defraud the people in pushing out the coin. When this end has been fully reached through the instrumentality of having control of the currency, they are enabled to enhance the value of the coin, and at the proper time they defraud them again, by the reversed process of re-acquiring the coin. These frauds are hid from the observation of the people through the complication of coinage and currency laws.

Since the discovery of the new mines, in California, Australia, Colorado and elsewhere, there has been a general expectation expressed in financial circles, that gold would depreciate, and some surprise has been manifested in some quarters, that this depreciation has not followed as was prophesied. That gold has fallen in actual value, there can be little doubt—the largely increased production would surely produce that result, if nothing intervened to prevent it. But, that intervention has occurred, in the form of the mint regulations of the world, and gold has so far been held up to the mint standard.

The people, however, are wronged in this, that the increased value given to gold by these laws does not add to the actual value of the gold, but their property is obtained at a proportionally less rate, and the only way that the industrial classes are made to feel effects of these wrongs, instead of learning the cause, is in the decreased comforts which they enjoy, and the increased burdens they have to bear.

These are the means, whereby the named and the unnamed nobility of the world are supported by law. The question then, as to the remedy to be applied, can only be satisfactorily settled by a clear understanding of all the agencies employed in exchanging property, and in estimating its value and amount. In this enquiry, as we have seen, the money of account holds a central position, and the effort, therefore, has been to place the subject in its true light.

In 1816, the British government under the influence of a very elaborate Report, made by the Earl of Liverpool, determined, that the pound sterling, their money of account, should be represented in a coin. They accordingly ordered a coin to be issued from the mint composed of five penny-weights, three grains and $\frac{171}{623}$ of a grain. Let those who ignore a money of account, as the real method of estimating values, show why a sovereign contains precisely this amount and quality of gold, if it was not to represent the pound sterling in a British coin.

The mistake, however, in attaching this numeral of value to a certain quantity and quality of gold, is the danger of depreciation in the value of gold, and the injury which will ensue by this arbitrary attempt to hold the price of gold up to the coinage level, when the actual, or market value of the gold, if left to seek its own level by its use, would be fifty or a hundred per cent. below the mint price level. As under the law every person is obliged to receive this gold at the mint value, and not at the market value. If gold should depreciate by increased production, one hundred per cent., and all the annual surplus productions of England, should be converted into this gold, at the mint price, the people of England would by law be cheated a hundred per cent., unless they can trade off the cheat to some-by else; and, although it has to a great extent been done, and the injury which has originated from this cause is very little understood. Yet, the wrong exists, and it is working results detrimental to the interests of the working classes, that cannot at present be estimated.

Upon such gross injustice is the uniform value of gold and silver erected, and nations continue to wallow in the mud and mire of iniquity to support the ruling classes, by this false system, and thereby to defraud and rob the industrial classes out of the just rewards of their honest toil In modern times England takes the lead in this systemized robbery. She is the centre of monopoly, and by this financial policy, she makes all nations pay her annual tribute of all their industries. The sun, it is boasted, never ceases to shine upon her dominion of gold. The United States, with all her vast resources, are first and foremost to follow in her wake, and seem only ambitious to exhaust her untold millions of natural wealth, and to impoverish the labor classes, that she may crown her republican institutions, by making them a first class centralized English money power.

This subject, however, will be more fully unfolded under the heads of coinage and banking.

The plea for these outrages is, that coinage is necessary to fix a standard of value, whereas, it has been seen, that this use, if it ever existed, since the dawn of civilization has long ago ceased, and that these important uses are performed by moneys of account.

By an act of Congress, passed on the 2d April, A. D. 1792, it is enacted: "That the money of account of the United States, shall be expressed in dollars, or units, dismes, [dimes] or tenths, cents or hundredths, and milles, [mills] or thousandths, a disme, [dime,] being the tenth part of a dollar; a cent, the hundredth part of a dollar; a mille, [mill,] the thousandth part of a dollar, and that all accounts in the public offices, and all proceedings in the courts of the United States, shall be kept and had in conformity to this regulation." United States Statutes at large, Sess. 1, Chap. 16, page 250.

Robert Morris, of Pennsylvania, financier of the confederation, on the 15th January, 1782, made a Report to Congress upon the subject of establishing a mint. This Report was not acted upon, but the subject was referred to Alexander Hamilton, Secretary of the Treasury, in April 1790, and on the 28th January, 1791, Hamilton made an elaborate Report. See American State papers Vol. VII. fol. ed. p. 91.

No coinage of any importance had ever existed in the Colonies. Spanish coins had been extensively used, but the money of account was very much deranged. Merchants were constantly using Spanish coins in making payments, and estimating their value in colonial pounds, shillings, and pence. This was extremely inconvenient, and a general desire was felt for having a uniform system, after the Revolution. Mr. Morris wanted to retain the colonial moneys of account; he well understood the difficulty with which a people change their mental habits, in estimating values; he, therefore, proposed a unit for the contemplated coinage, which would be a common *divisor* for all the moneys of account of the different States. This *divisor* was the 1,440th part of a dollar, divided as follows:

10 units to be equal to one penny
10 pence "   "   " bit
10 bits   "   "   " dollar
10 dollars "   "   " crown.

Under this division of the dollar, 24 parts would constitute a penny of Georgia—15, one of New York and North Carolina—20, of Virginia and the New England States, and 16, of Pennsylvania and the middle States. This dollar would have been two-thirds the value of the Spanish dollar. But Mr. Hamilton was of the opinion, that the people by the constant use of the Spanish dollar were better prepared for the adoption of the dollar unit of a money of account, and Mr. Jefferson, coinciding, the money of account, here given, was adopted. State papers, Finance Vol. II. page 105—Vol. VII. page 105.

This, it is believed, is the first time a money of account was ever adopted by legislative enactment. It is now thoroughly incorporated into the mental habits of the people; all that is required to preserve this mode of reckoning intact, is first, a repeal of all coinage and banking-laws, second, the institution of a national money, agreeing in denominations with this money of account, stamped upon paper, or some convenient and durable material, having only an immaterial value, made a legal equivalent for all property, by being made a legal tender for all debts, or obligations, public and private ; its legal properties, or attributes, being understood by the people, will secure its uniform value, by the uses it performs It being a universal equivalent for all property, yet divested of its commodity value, it will not be obliged to fluctuate with the market value of commodities, or of any one commodity, but will represent these changes in the market with unerring certainty. In short, it will be the greenback and our money of account perfected and perpetuated. It will only cease when the government ceases, or when justice and equity shall no longer be regarded by the government or nation.

CHAPTER II.

COINAGE—ITS USES AND ABUSES.

There is no question pertaining to money and its uses, upon which there rests a more profound mystery in the popular mind, than that relating to gold and silver. Their uniformity of value, their supposed control over the market, in regulating prices, or in determining the value of all other commodities, and there is none, upon which there has been written more arrant nonsense.

If savans upon financial science are to be believed, the Creator it seems must have exhausted all his wisdom, and put forth his creative powers to the uttermost, to hide deep in the bowels of the earth, the *precious metals*, as they are called, in order that man, on a scale correspondingly grand, might be able to find a reliable measure of value, a standard of value, and a representative of value. Yet at the very next breath, it is proclaimed, that it is labor, and not silver and gold, which settles the price of everything; that it costs so much labor to raise a bushel of wheat, to manufacture a yard of cloth, or to dig an ounce of gold or silver—therefore after all, the great regulator of value is labor.

But giving to all these wonderful claims their due weight—just how much value should be attached to each and to the whole; can best be determined by an accurate analysis of the qualities and uses of these metals—this will show how much is to be credited to intrinsic worth, and how much to legal attributes and absurd customs.

For with all their immense power, like all other commodities, their value depends upon use, but unlike all others, that use is very much enlarged by unjust and wicked monopolizing laws.

In the preceding chapter it has been seen that in no correct sense are coins—measures, standards, or representatives of value, but simply legal standards of payment.

As a nation, we are almost entirely indebted to the enactment of a money of account passed by Congress in 1792 for modes of reckoning, as well as for the extirpation of the several colonial moneys of account, but even these, as has been shown, did not owe their origin to either gold or silver coin.

The Spanish dollars, however, furnished material aid in preparing the way for the establishment of our unit of a money of account, but its decimals were taken from the Arabic numerals.

It will be very readily seen that the use of these numerals of value, or the unit and its decimal parts of the money of account, in keeping books, in naming prices, estimating values in the ordinary transactions of business, and in process, judgements, and decrees of courts, would add more than a thousand to one over coin. in fixing a knowledge of this denominational mode of reckoning. Besides, notwithstanding the mint regulation made gold and silver coin a legal standard of payment, yet in every days business transactions, a currency which is clearly illegal, has taken the place of coin in making payments; even when legal tenders have been made in this currency, if no objection was made at time of the tender, the courts have sustained it.

In this manner, coin has been dispensed with, in business channels, and we may congratulate ourselves not so much in once having had a coin, as that we have escaped the intolerable evil of a debased coinage, and thus the way is now open for getting rid of this labor robbing system.

The mere fact that man in the early and barbaric ages of the world, may have made his exchanges by comparing one thing with another, or that in this barter stage of trade, measurement of quantity became a necessity in determining the value of one commodity, with a view to ascertaining the value of other commodities, and so far as gold and silver are concerned, a public certificate of quantity and quality, may be as necessary now, as it has been in any other period of the world. But, as has already been shown, it by no means follows that the measurement of values is made by the legal standard of payment, of so many grains of silver or gold, because the statute has fixed this arbitrary mode of payment. Nor does it follow, that because 232 grains of fine gold makes a coin of ten dollars, called an eagle, that, therefore, when the market determines that a certain quantity of wheat is worth ten dollars, the wheat is gold or silver dollars, or that it is measured by the coin. Nor does it thence follow, that the term dollars, *ex vi termini*, means gold or silver dollars. Yet, such is the logic of the popular idea of coinage, and all the teachings of those who make *lawful* gain by this iniquitous law, and of those who write in their interest.

MacLeod, in his treatise on banking, says, that " when nations advanced beyond the stage of direct barter and began to use the *precious metals*, as a common measure, to which the value of all other commodities was referred, it was the weight of the *pure metal*, which was invariably used as the index of value, and merchants carried scales about with them for the purpose of weighing out the metals on each separate occasion. The necessity of carrying about scales to weigh out the metal, on each separate occasion, being felt to be tedious and irksome, the plan was devised of cutting the bullion into pieces of a certain definite weight by the public authority, and putting a stamp upon them to certify to the community that they were warranted to contain a certain weight of bullion, of a certain definite fineness. Values were then estimated by the number of these pieces of bullion which were called coins, which were given for commodities, and they were said to be reckoned by *tale* "—that is by count. He then says : " It is clear that the sole object of coinage was to save the trouble of weighing, and that though the prices of articles were estimated in figures, it was *essentially* a part of the understanding that these figures denote a certain specific quantity of pure metal." MacLeod Theory and Practice of Banking Vol. I. pp. 275—276.

Undoubtedly this is correct where men are dealing in the gold itself. But if this was the essential object of coinage; when the quantity and quality had been determined and duly authenticated, why not stop at this point. If that was all that is involved in these mint regulations, and kindred laws, no objection could be made to them ; but such is not the point where they are anchored.

These laws go further, and they are potent instrumentalities for deranging prices, and the most powerful engine of oppression which the state can erect. Not only are the quantity and quality of these metals determined by coinage laws, but they lay impious hands upon the laws governing values, seizing upon the market value at some period of time, no matter what the market value thereafter may be, the coin is held up to the point of value thus fixed by the mint regulations of the world.

Around this coinage dagon the industrial classes, their property, and their rights must dance to the music, and keep time to suit the interest of the gold-gamblers, stock-jobbers and bankers, for whose special benefit these laws are enacted.

For it will be readily seen that there is no good reason why gold and silver should be a legal tender, at a fixed price, any more than any other commodities.

But, by such legal enactments not only are the natural laws of supply and demand thereby annulled, and destroyed, in the use of these metals, but an artificial demand for their use is thus created, with which under the natural laws governing commerce, it is frequently impossible to comply without spreading broadcast disaster and ruin to every commercial and industrial interest.

The coinage system is built upon the idea that commerce instead of being an instrumentality for benefitting man, by so arranging the distribution of products, that the article sold, shall in the easiest and best manner pay for the article bought, must be made to refer to some one common equivalent for all articles, and thereby the mutual exchange of articles must be regulated, not by the law of supply and demand, governing the production and sale of the commodities, but the law governing the demand and supply of gold and silver.

In this manner, the interest of the financiers, capitalists, gold-gamblers and stock-jobbers, are created and protected, while the whole industrial and useful business is plundered and robbed.

Take away then from gold and silver the shield of law contained in these various mint regulations, in the uses of these metals which flow from the system, and it would be difficult to determine, either, their value or ultimate use.

It is very certain, however, that if governments would content themselves with the enactment of laws to protect the public against imposition in the quantity and qualities of these metals, and leave the people to deal, or not to deal in, or use them as their inclination may prompt, it would be one important step in the right direction.

This meddlesome legislation pre-supposes, that the masses of men are an ignorant, barbarian crowd, fit only to be protected, that they may be plundered by the State. Its origin dates at that period when it was thought, that the Church, or State, should determine what a man's religion should be; and if the State was competent to provide for the salvation of men's souls, surely it was competent to provide for, and regulate their business to teach them what to do, and how to do it.

Under this soul-saving and business-directing theory, gold and silver held the most prominent place. The dazzling brilliance of royalty, lies in silks and satins, ornamented with necklaces, ear nose and finger rings, of gold and silver.

Hence originated the absurd idea that every transaction in commerce is a losing one, which does not bring to the country engaging in it a surplus of gold and silver.

Out of these absurd ideas, based on an inordinate love of gain, mint regulations originated, and to answer these purposes of gain, from age to age, they have been perpetuated.

If by increased production, these metals should actually be depreciated one hundred per cent., mint regulations still hold the price that much above their actual value.

If by war, or any other similar cause, the productions of a country are decreased so much as to produce an increase of the price of labor and of products a hundred per cent., then a paper money and the coin mark that variation—the paper by an increased number of dollars to be paid, and the gold and silver by premiums. The governments pay the increased value of the coin, as a commodity, in bonds, at a hundred per cent. discount, with interest, and the capitalist, under this system, will require the fifty dollars he furnished the government, to be replaced by a hundred dollars, and interest, and to be taken out of the people's earnings.

Not only this, but there are also supposed legal obligations arising out of the mere use of the denominational terms—dollars, pounds, etc., which bind burdens upon mens' shoulders too grievous to be borne.

One fiction of this class is, "that when one man lends another a sum of *money* to be returned to him at some future period.... in the eye of the law—" he grants," it is said, "the use of a certain number of pieces of metal of given weight and fineness, during a definite period, on condition that an equal number of pieces of metal of the same weight and fineness shall be restored, at the expiration of the time. There is no question of value, or what quantity of commodities, or set of commodities the gold will command in exchange. This has no part in the contract, the agreement respects the *quantity*, and not the value of the gold; it has nothing to do with the purchasing power of the gold in the market."

"This is a correct representation of all *mere* pecuniary bargains. We must come to a *quantity* of something, at last." MacLeod, Vol. I. page 289.

Now, dealing is supposed to be for the purpose of exchanging an article which a man does not want, for something that he does want.

What good purpose can be subserved in carrying out this object, to send thousands of men down into the bowels of the earth; to dig out the precious metals not for the purpose of being used in those departments of business where they are useful, or necessary, but merely to create a beautiful and costly medium of exchange; to enable the people to convert their hogs, sheep and turkeys, into gold, which they do not want, for the purpose of changing this into oxen, cows, and horses, which they do want.

Or, why should it be deemed necessary, that when a man sells a hundred hogs for one thousand dollars, at ninety days, to imagine that this change can only be effected through the medium of so many grains of gold, or silver, and thus, that it is necessary " to come to a quantity of something, at last."

All this, it must borne in mind, flows from the mere technical signification of the terms—dollars, pounds. Yet, no dollars, or pounds, are actually used, or required to be used; and all this imaginary use of gold and silver, when paper only is used, is in every contract for the payment of money.

Moran, in his treatise on money, says: " Coins are mere pieces of metal of fixed weight, and quality, tested by an authority recognized by all, with which purchases may be made, and all contracts for the payment of *money* fulfilled. A contract to pay one thousand dollars, pounds, florins, francs, or any other coin, is simply a contract to deliver a certain number of pieces of metal of a certain weight and fineness; and the coins are such pieces certified correct by certain authority.

How unjust then, how great the abuse of power for a government to debase the coin, or to make paper a legal tender, and thus force creditors to accept in liquidation of existing contracts, something else than what the contract stipulated." Moran, page 27 and 28.

No doubt, a contract for the delivery of so many pieces of gold and silver of a certain specified weight and quality should be fulfilled by the delivery of the article specified, the same as any other contract—but that is a very different question from that which would make the mere use of the denominational terms— dollars, pounds and livres to mean coin. If the obligor is legally required to pay coin, or its equivalent every time these terms are mentioned, it is well not only to understand the fact, but also why it is so, and what is the object of such a construction of language, when no coin is intended, or generally used.

The currency in this country, and in England, for the last hundred years has been paper, and the term dollars, pounds, and livres, or francs, have had in practice only a denominational signification, the same as in the case of numerals. Why should there be any legal construction of the contract, requiring payment in coin, when the terms used apply to the money of account, equally, as well as to coin, and when not a thousandth part of the business of the country is a coin deal; and generally, to enforce such a law, would ruin both, the industrial and commercial interests of the country.

A legal tender should be made to denote all classes of property, but should not permit any one species of property to be used. If property is used at all, it should be all kinds of property, and at market price.

No such perversion of the use of denominational units is permitted, in any other department of science, or business, where similar terms are used.

Three barley coins make one inch, and twelve inches one foot. Does a contract for a thousand feet of lumber, though the quantity is estimated by feet, and expressed in numerals, or figures, imply that it was an essential part of the understanding, that these figures denote an actual measurement with barleycorns? Again, four inches make one hand; A. sells B. a horse sixteen hands high—is it a part of the bargain that the horse is sixteen hands high, measured by 192 barley-corns? There is a difference in the length of barley-corns; 192, might make the horse thirteen high—at other times sixteen.

Another illustration: The Arabic mode of notation has ten characters, nine of which have a certain power or value of their own—the tenth, of itself, has no value, but when placed at the right hand side of any number it increases the unit power of each unit in a tenfold ratio. Now these arabic numbers are called digits, from fingers. Is there any implied understanding that these numerals, with the nought, or zero, receive their power in every instance from the visible presence of fingers, as derived from their origin? But are not the barley-corns and the fingers as essential to quantity, and its measurement, as it is that these money-numerals shall actually denote a certain quantity of pure metal, every time the denominational term dollars is used? Why are capitalists and bankers, so tenacious on this point? They never use coin, to any considerable extent, except as a commodity—as they do not furnish coin, why do they demand it from their debtors? Is it a question of public good, or private gain? The following illustration may throw some light upon this dark subject. A. is a rich banker, or capitalist, is the principal shareholder in the Merchants Bank of the City of New York, it⁕ has a capital of ten millions of dollars, its stockholders have actually paid in one per cent. of its capital in gold. The government desires a loan of $5,000,000. A. is the principal stockholder, owns two-thirds of this immense capital—controls the bank, being exceedingly patriotic he takes the whole loan, exchanges his five millions of promises to pay, bearing no interest, for the well secured $5,000,000 of National bonds, bearing six per cent. gold, interest, payable semi-annually—and the principal in twenty years after date, at the time of this loan the prices current in the interest and under the control of capitalists, quote A.'s money, or currency, at par, and gold, at 250 premium. The term dollars in this bond of the Government means so many pieces of coin, of a certain quantity of pure metal. " We must come to a quantity of something at last."

To fulfill the solemn obligations of the Government to A. for the period of twenty years, requires the following amount :

Of standard coin, to wit, principal......$5,000,000
Int. on the same.................... 6,000,000
Cost of collecting, say three per cent.... 330,000
_____
Total.....................$11,330,000

This certainly presents a strong pecuniary interest in favor of having " dollars " always mean so much gold or silver coin, of a certain quality and weight. And when special class interests are created, the plastic hand of justice soon moulds judicial decision into such unity with these pecuniary class interests that a pre-established harmony dwells only with partial laws, and there seems to be no antagonism anywhere, but in the frail and conflicting rights belonging to the people.

There are so many ways in which these mints regulations enable men to gain not only a living, but amass vast fortunes without performing useful service, that it is useless to attempt to give any thing more than an outline of the subject without writing a large octavo.

If the actual worth of the precious metals of the world be estimated at $4,000,000,000, and coinage increases the value 40 per cent., which is probably a very low estimate, this would amount to $1,600,000,000. The enhanced value of the metals does not add to their useful properties, but to their purchasing power.

The extent of the derangement to business thus caused cannot be estimated.

It is easy to discover that the much boasted and loudly proclaimed uniformity of value and the unusual use of these metals, are from this source. It is not use nor intrinsic value which produces these results, but it is for the purposes of commercial gain, and for securing political power, by which this gross wrong is, from age to age, perpetuated.

The derangement of prices and the effects of mint regulations are best exhibited on the theatre of war, on a large scale, like that of our late conflict. To illustrate this let a parallel between wheat and gold be instituted. Before the war gold stood at, say from one to two per cent. premium, and wheat, in the seaboard marts, was par at a $1.50 per bushel. War sweeps its devastating course over the land, and wheat goes up to $2.50, perhaps to $3.00 per bushel, and gold goes up to 290—300. What creates the difference in the market price of this and all other commodities as compared with gold?

If wheat is shipped abroad it may not bring as much as before the war, but gold being held by the mint regulation to its former level is therefore the article at a large premium to be exported. The foreign nation, if it is not a lender, will soon be so gorged with gold that it cannot be loaned at exceeding one or two per cent., as has lately occurred in London and Paris. While in the country at war, increased and irregular prices will soon manifest themselves in suddenly emerged millionaires with a plentiful crop of pauperism and crime.

War itself would have, it is true, this desolating effect, but its miseries as well as its origin, are more than trebled by this fruitful instrumentality.

To illustrate the false principle of coinage still more forcibly, let the principle be applied to some one of the agricultural products, for instance to wheat. Suppose all nations should make a bushel of wheat a legal tender at two dollars per bushel. Such a connected series of laws, if universally enforced, would not only enhance the value of wheat, but correspondingly depreciate all other commodities, as compared with wheat. Yet, taking labor and property together, the price of the whole would be increased the extent to which such a law could be made to operate, though it would be at very unequal rates, proportioned to the excess of supply or demand, in each department of industry or business.

Labor being the great regulator of value, increased price of any product for consumption, whether from natural causes or artificial regulations will increase the price of labor and its products.

The increased price of the wheat, in consequence of the legal tender laws, would be but a small share of the injury inflicted.

The storage of large quantities of wheat, for the mere purpose of settling balances, would, to that extent, take from the people the benefits of the natural uses of the grain, which loss would have to be supplied by more expensive agencies. But the wrongs thus imposed would bear no comparison with the injuries inflicted by coinage laws, for the reason that gold and silver are extremely limited in amount, and cannot be rapidly increased.

If, however, there is a lingering doubt still remaining, that it is not mint regulations, but the natural demand for these metals which gives their efficiency as well as uniformity of value, why do they not bear a uniform price all over the world? In England and in this country the ratable value of silver, as compared to gold, is about fifteen and a half to one less than gold, while in Japan one ounce of gold is only worth three and a half ounces of silver. In 1856, there was a drain of silver from Europe of $100,739,605, to answer the demands of the trade with Asia, an amount more than double the yield of all the mines of Europe and America for a single year.

The exportations of silver from France, for the year 1852, up to 1859, inclusive, exceeded the importations by 1,378,862,000 francs ($275,750,000.) Whilst the exportations of silver from England and the Mediterranean ports for China and the East Indies, during those years were 1,917,500,000 francs, 76½ per cent. of the entire exports from France. This demonstrates not only the effect which mint regulations have in determining the value of these metals, but the damaging effect which flows from tying money to coinage, in order to enable men to deal with the despots of Asia—or Europe either.

The apprehensions of a fall in gold, and a rise in silver, occasioned by this drain, induced the Bank of France, and other large holders of silver, to refuse to exchange with the English silver for gold, at par, and England was thus forced to resort to the money changers of the continent to obtain silver, upon which they had to pay a premium, to enable them to liquidate the balance of trade with Asia, occasioned by the demand under their laws making silver a legal equivalent, instead of gold.

Having, as is believed, explained and illustrated the arbitrary and unjust principles of coinage, as connected with the business affairs of every day life, far enough to give a just idea of the control, and of the damaging effect which flows from it, it is now proposed to examine it as a principle of power, connected with, and developed by Kings or Sovereigns—a more fearful history of outrage and wrong cannot be given.

Through this potent instrumentality for unnumbered centuries, the iron heel of despotism has been firmly planted upon the necks, and deeply imbedded into the living flesh, of earth's toiling millions. Its pathway has been through fields of blood. But the time has come at last when the people begin to demand a reason for this tyrannical sway. They desire to know the secret of its power, and every link of the golden chain must be inspected and weighed, before the tyrant can be dethroned.

Gold and silver was first coined by the Lydians at the close of the ninth century B. C., and by Greece proper at the close of the eighth. William the Conqueror issued no coins, but silver premiums or sterlings. Henry III. coined gold pennies $\frac{1}{120}$ of a pound tower for 20d. Henry VII. first coined silver shillings. Silver half pence and farthings were coined from the time of Edward I. to Edward VI. The first copper coinage in England was under Charles II. in 1672. Henry the VII. coined the first sovereigns of gold, 23 carats, 3½ fine, in 1489. In 1544, Henry VIII. coined half, quarter and eighth sovereigns, of the present standard of 22 carats fine.

Charles II. coined the first African gold, in 1675, and from this circumstance the coin was called a Guinea. Nearly, if not all of the sovereigns of Europe falsified the moneys they coined, by decreasing the weight and fineness of the metal. This fraudulent act was done to enable them to pay their debts by this dishonest practice.

In the Roman Empire, 550 B. C., in the reign of Servius

Tullius, the *as* or *pondo* contained a Roman pound of copper; in 175, B. C., it had been reduced to $\frac{1}{2}$ oz., or $\frac{1}{24}$ part of its original weight.

In France, under Charlemagne, the livre contained twelve ounces of pure silver. It was reduced by his successors, Philip le Bel, and the first sovereigns of the house of Valois. There was seventy-one alterations in the coin in nine years by John the Good. By edict of Nov. 27th, 1359, the marc of pure silver were coined into 18 livres, by that of January 22d, 1360, into 54 livres—March 22, 1360, into 125, and so on to the end of the chapter. These changes, whether lowered or raised, were the source of enormous wrongs and frauds. The subject was not only cheated by the sovereign, but subjects were thus licensed or compelled to cheat each other. This debasement of the coin continued till the reign of Louis XV. From 1497 to 1602, the livre was reduced from 2.225 to 1.208 centigrammes of pure silver. In 1789, the livre contained $\frac{1000}{1835}$ of the pure silver, that it did in the reign of Charlemagne. Journal des Economistes, Paris, September, 1862, p. 372, 373—Moran p. 12.

Henry the VIII. was the first sovereign in England who debased the sterling value of the coin. The shilling of William the Conqueror, contained $266\frac{4}{5}$ grains tower, or $249\frac{3}{4}$ grains troy of pure silver; it was reduced by Edward VI., in 1550, to $21\frac{1}{8}$ grains tower, or 20 grains troy. The English mint used the tower pound until the 18th Henry VII., when it was replaced by the troy pound, which is $\frac{3}{4}$ of an oz. heavier.

The following table shows the changes of value in the silver coinage of England:

	Standard or fine silver in pound of 12 oz.	Standard silver coined into		Grains Troy of stand. sil. in one penny	Grains Troy of fine silver in one penny
		per lb Tower	per lb. Troy		
Conquest A. D. 1066	11. oz. 2 dwt.	20 s. 0 d		22½	20.81...
28 Edward L A. D. 1300	do do	20 3		22¼	20.55...
18 Edward III. A. D. 1344	do do	22 2		20¼	18.69...
20 do do do 1346	do do	22 6		20	18.50...
25 do do do 1350	do do	25 6		18	16.65...
+3 Henry IV. do 1412	do do	30 0		15	13.87...
c4 Edward IV. do 1464	do do	37 6		12	11.10...
+8 Henry VIII. do 1526	do do	42 2¼	45 s. 0 d	10¾	9.87...
34 do do do 1543	10 oz. 0 dwt.		48 0	10	8.33...
36 do do do 1544	6 do do		48 0	10	5.—...
37 do do do 1545	4 do do		48 0	10	3.33...
3 Edward VI. do 1549	6 do do		72 0	6⅔	3.33...
4 do do do 1550	3 do do		72 0	6⅔	1.67...
6 do do do 1552	11 do 1		60 0	8	7.37...
1 Elizabeth do 1558	11 do 2		60 0	8	7.50 ..
3 do do 1601	11 do 2		62 0	7⅜	7.16...
6 George III. do 1816	11 do 2		64 0	7¼	6.727

Thus it is seen, that during eight hundred years, the gold

standard measure of England, under kings and parliaments was a cheat and fraud of the most stupenduous character, involving the rights and the interests of the industrial and business classes of that great nation, making these in fact the mere dice of royalty and its retainers

Pure gold is 24 carats fine. The carat is an Abyssinian weight divided into 4 grains, the grains into quarters. A carat grain is equivalent to 2½ dwts. The English mint standard of gold for their coin at first was 23¼ carats, 3½ grains fine, and ¼ grain alloy, this continued to be the standard until 18 Henry VII. who then introduced a new standard of 22 carats fine and 2 carats alloy. Both these standards were used by him and his success-sors until 1633. From that period to the present they have been 22 carats fine. Standard gold has ever since 1717, been coined into £3. 17s. 10½ per oz. By the act of 1844, the Bank of Eng-land, as has been shown, is obligated to purchase all the gold bullion and foreign coins of standard fineness, at £3. 17s. 9d. per oz.

Debasement of coins was universal during the middle ages. In Scotland, previous to 1296, the pound of silver was coined into 20 shillings. In 1601, £36, or 720 shillings were coined out of the same quantity. The gold ducat, or sequin, when first coined, in Venice, in 1284, was equivalent to 3 Italian livres; to-day it would be worth 22 livres. The florin, originally a gold coin of the value of about 20 shillings sterling, ($2.50,) is now a silver coin worth about 20 pence sterling, (40 cents.) The Spanish coin, maravedi, in 1220, weighed 24 grammes, (370) grains troy of gold ; it is now a small coin equal to $\frac{44}{373}$ of an English penny. The Russian rouble of 1700, is worth $2\frac{70}{100}$ of the roubles of 1821.

But besides, the kings not satisfied with the gains made by the frauds committed in changing the value of the coin, naturally went to robbing. Charles the Second, robbed the bankers, or goldsmiths of a large sum of money, on two occasions. It had been deposited in the exchequer for safe keeping, where he seized it, and appropriated it to his own use. The amount taken was £1,328,520, or in dollars, $6,642,650, a large amount for that period.

Charles the First, at one time seized £200,000, deposited in the mint, and Charles the Second, robbed one banker of £416,722.

These frauds and robberies constitute but a small share of the wrongs and outrages perpetuated through the coinage system. Its accumulation in large amounts is the inevitable result of making it a legal tender for settling balances—this invited robbery, royal and otherwise. This catalogue of crime may be summed up as follows: largely increased value, debasement of the coin and robbery are the natural fruits of the system. That governments have no right to fix the price of labor is generally admitted. Yet the wrong inflicted by such an act would bear no comparison with the one which arbitrarily fixes the price of any one commodity, thus making it a medium for controlling, and at the same time of deranging the price of every other commodity, or service.

Yet the plea that is put forth for the continuation of this outrage is, that other nations have adopted coinage as a common medium of exchange, and therefore, that we in order to deal with them must follow in their wake. A very little sober reflection will show the fallacy of this argument. Mint regulations have no force beyond the nation by which such laws are enacted. Our coinage will not affect the value of the metals abroad, their laws, not ours, will govern. If these laws increase the value of the metal we shall to that extent be benefitted. If, on the other hand, the market value depends upon the law of supply and demand, then intrinsic qualities of the metal for use under this law will control the value, so that under any view which can be taken, coinage laws are unnecessary. All that is required is to authenticate or stamp the weight and quality of the metal by national authority.

Coinage and mint regulations for the home market are as unnecessary and mischievous as every other law would be, which attempts to regulate values by arbitrary enactments, instead of permitting the law of supply and demand to control. And we have not, and probably never will have, coin adequate for one-twentieth part of the business of the country. If we had, as gold and silver are commodities, they cannot be held in sufficient quantities to supply the money as well as the market demand for their use.

Besides, the cost of coinage is a serious obstacle in the way of circulating coin. In England, coinage of gold costs one-half of one per cent., and silver probably one and a half per cent. In France gold costs 0.193 per cent—silver 75 centimes for every 100 francs, or $\frac{3}{4}$ per cent. In Russia, gold costs $\frac{8.5}{100}$ per cent., and silver $2\frac{7}{65}$. While in the United States the estimated expense of coinage of all metals is as follows :

At Philadelphia................$2\frac{23}{100}$ per cent.
New Orleans................$6\frac{91}{100}$ " "
North Carolina................9 " "
Georgia......................$9\frac{91}{100}$ " "

Thus it will be seen that in the United States the cost of coinage is much larger than elsewhere, and more than double the cost which would be necessary to furnish a paper circulation upon a just business basis. No account is taken, either, of the waste of metal, in coining, nor of its rapid wearing out by use. Then again, we are a commercial people, our coins would not only flow out, but the coin of other nations would soon flow in, and like all other nations who have tried the experiment, we should find the market flooded with the diverse depreciated, and oftentimes counterfeit foreign coin.

In the commercial portions of Europe while coinage was at the zenith of its glory, their marts of trade were flooded with a diversified coin like those of Germany and Italy, business men were obliged to resort to the patriarchical mode of making payments by scales. Tables had to be constructed of the various coins in circulation, and their respective values designated in the money of account of the place where they were to be used.

In Kelly's Cambist (page 154) is the copy of a table, made by Sir Isaac Newton, in the same volume several of recent date may be found. These tables show that there were thirty gold coins called ducats, twenty-five of which were from different mints, with different impressions. Scarcely any two of which were of the same value. There were twenty-three gold coins called pistoles, from nineteen different mints, differing in value and impression. No less than fifty-one coins, called rix-dollars, were in circulation from twenty different mints, and of varying value.

This enumeration of coins, comprises but a small portion compared with the whole of Europe—much less compared with the coinage of the world. It is sufficient to show the character of the difficulty arising from a diversified coinage, though giving no adequate idea of the doubt and difficulty introduced into business by the use of *standard measures* of value.

These royal robberies and frauds, multiplied, and diverse coin bearing the same name, differing widely in value, counterfeiting, sweating, filing, plugging and cheating on *private* account, the dangers of robbery in holding and transporting, together with the loss occasioned by the natural wear of coin from incessant handling, were prominent among the causes which led to a universal use of the moneys of account, or ideal moneys of the banks of Venice, Genoa, Amsterdam and Hamburg. Business men were glad to find a refuge in these, from the intolerable evils of coinage. The bank money of Venice, for five hundred years bore a premium over coin, averaging over twenty per cent.

Colwell, in his admirable work, thus sums up the evils of the coinage system: " The history of coinage, for nearly ten centuries, is a history of public frauds and private injuries, of confusion in prices, and in moneys of account, of immense gains as well as losses by governments, and still heavier losses without gains by the people. These mischiefs may be credited without hesitation to the continued effort to maintain a fixed price and forced circulation for coins, and to the fraudulent debasements to which these efforts opened a door, and afforded a temptation. This history affords no lessons more worth remembering than that governments should not, and cannot, *fix the price of the precious metals, even in coins*, beyond the demand for the retail trade ; that there should not be any other price for the precious metals, whether coined or uncoined, in the large transactions of commerce, than that which is made by the law of prices, and the course of trade. The history of money, [coin,] shows that few greater grievances can befall a people than a deranged coinage, and money of account; few evils have drawn from the masses of a nation more bitter complaints. But for the great advantage of coins in small transactions, it had been better that no mint had ever existed." Colwell, page 138.

Experience, however, demonstrates that even in small change, paper is more convenient than coin; the only difficulty is its rapid destruction by use. Some easier and better mode for changing the soiled and worn fractional currency, is all that is required to make it much better than coin.

The history of coinage is far from showing either uniformity of value or use, much less does it show that its use has been beneficial.

The use of representatives of value is coeval with the history of the race—but the material used has by no means been uniform. Salt is used in Abyssinia. Codfish in Iceland and Newfoundland. Slaves and oxen were used by the Anglo-Saxons—

Westminster Review, Janury 1st, 1848. Iron was used by Lycurgus and his successors, for some five hundred years. Tobacco in Virginia. Corn and wheat in Massachusetts. Leather by the Carthagenians. The bark of the mulberry tree in China, and notched sticks were used as exchequer bills, in England as late as at the beginning of the 18th century. Finally, the whole system in Europe and America, has culminated in the use of paper almost entirely, for all the practical purposes of making an exchange, and gold and silver are used merely as commodities, in settling balances—and there is just as good reason for going back to barbarism, and adopting any other barbaric mode of exchange, as there is for continuing the use of coin. To avoid the endless weighing process, coinage was adopted. The state then used it as an engine of power, oppression, fraud, outrage, and wrong, to escape from these intolerable evils paper representatives have been substituted. But the principle adopted being the same, as that which underlies coinage, all the frauds and robberies inflicted by a debased coinage have been more than preserved under the paper representative system. A double fraud is now thereby inflicted upon the people.

There is no other remedy for these accumulated evils, but by a repeal of all currency, coinage, and gold bond laws—and the institution of a paper money based upon property, and not any species of property, and under the absolute management and control of the State.

Whatever contracts may have been made, requiring payment in coin, should be settled at the earliest possible period, and no legislation should be permitted by the American people, which through the instrumentality of money and bonds looks to the further support and building up of a moneyed class by the Government, at the expense of the industrial classes.

CHAPTER III.

MONEY—A LEGALIZED AGENT.

The vague, indefinite ideas which men generally entertain as to the proper mode of instituting a money, its functions and powers, arise not only from the want of attention to the subject on the part of the people, but there has been a studied design on the part of those benefitted by the system, to make these laws as intricate as possible, for the very purpose of not having them understood by any body, but themselves. In the charter to the Bank of England, there was no direct power granted, authorizing the Bank to issue paper or currency, and the real design of the institution was not understood until a long time after the passage of the law creating the Bank.

But the tendency of education, under these partial laws, and the false customs and habits of thought created by doing business through this channel, all point in the same direction. The concealment of the gross injustice contained in the laws instituting money, or that which is designed for, and is necessarily used as money.

Again, the isolation of men engaged in the industrial and useful occupations of life has in a great measure removed them from those channels of business and sources of thought which are necessary for forming accurate opinions upon this subject.

The power of money is artificial—not natural—legal—not just.

In all legitimate and natural occupations there is more or less connection between the service performed and the compensation bestowed. No arbitrary enactments, no special grants, nor partial laws *compel* labor, or regulate its rewards. But in the institution of money, the depletion of the many, and the enrichment of the few ; class and caste are the supreme objects of the law instituted, its rewards are mere arbitrary legal extortions, and its objects are simply diabolical or infernal.

In useful industry there is a natural demand and a natural use to be performed which is neither to be ignored or shirked. Its due performance is indispensible to the comfort of the individual, and the welfare of society—its rewards directly grow out of the service performed. Neither patents of nobility, nor charters of special privileges are necessary—the grant is from the Supreme, and the mandate to every son and daughter of Adam, is " in the sweat of thy face shall thou eat bread." It is this overshadowing obligation and sense of duty which with the masses of men, calls into exercise every mental and physical power. Every days necessities, and every days duties increases the responsibilities, and deepens the channel in which these thoughts run.

The obligation and the power thus exercised are *individual or personal*, not *legal, institutional, or aggregate.* Hence nothing is, or can be further removed from the mental philosophy of every day life than the unjust *legal* power, and unjust *legal* rewards allotted to the money class through these extremely partial laws.

The charter of every day life is justice in act. The charter of the money power is a special dispensation, which to the chosen few, annuls the conditions imposed upon the ignoble many. The love and practice of the former, is a necessity for the development and growth of humanity of the *latter*, is utterly to pervert and destroy it.

None of the "*many inventions*," devised by human wit, and human folly, have so effectually chilled the finer sensibilities of the human heart, and perverted its nobler powers to the worship of self as has this unjust institution of money.

No wonder that the Saviour of the world proclaimed it " easier for a camel to go through the eye of a needle, than for a rich man to enter the Kingdom of Heaven." No wonder that the apostle James declared that the "love of money is the root of all evil." No wonder either that men following the god-ordained and useful occupations of human society, and human life find it so difficult to comprehend its principles, or understand its manifold workings.

If the milennium is to dawn on earth, it must be long after the extinguishment of this unjust power, unless humanity shall find some new mode of development and progress, more rapid than any yet discovered.

How can it be expected that men who are licensed to break every natural law, and thus to violate the golden rule, will consent to be governed by its holy teachings. Why license a few men to charge a certain rent for their unsecured ŋo rent bearing promises, and require the people in return to give their well secured rent or interest bearing securities. What justice, human or divine, is that which thus commits to any class of men the right to use the sovereign power of the State for their own private gain, and to substitute their faithless promises in the place of what ought to be the lawful money of the State, and in addition to this to determine arbitrarily how much, or how little, a free people require to transact their business in making exchanges of property.

It is not the abuse of the banking or money power of the Government, which inflicts deadly harm to the best interests of society—the abuse is in the grant of power itself. It is based upon the ,assumption that the state has a right to abdicate sovereignty in favor of a class—that *money* instead of representing the property, justice and sovereignty of the people, should represent the interest, property, and sovereignty of the banker—instead of being made to enable·the people to make a just, easy, and cheap exchange of their property, is made to be hoarded up in the vaults of a bank to be used as a legalized commodity or agent to suit the convenience of bankers and financiers, either to redeem their faithless promises called "*currency*," or to otherwise fleece the people as the interest of the financial classes demand. But the people are beginning to enquire whether the value of this "currency" depends upon the *money* or bonds of the State, locked up in the bank, or upon the property of the people which it exchanges; and if upon the money or other security, then they they want to know why not circulate the money or security itself. If it depends upon the avails of their property, why pay the bankers for plundering them? What additional security do they add to the money, or to the bonds, or what security does their bank paper furnish? Is it in the intrinsic quality of the paper or beauty of design, or is it in the splendid autographs of soulless corporation officials? These—all these have furnished no security in the past. What indemnity do they promise for the future? Where and what is the present actual value of the currency as based upon a present ability to redeem out of the bankers and financiers own property? or where or what is the security to the people for their deposites, and the echo of a thousand years answers, where? The prophet's vision of the valley of dry bones may resurrect and clothe them with living flesh, but it can never resurrect the departed millions lost by bank failures—return the lost deposites, or restore to the people their long betrayed rights—these under the banking regime are never to be restored. The only infallible remedy for these wrongs is the institution of money upon principles of justice, to be administered under the direct control of the Government. The first and most important question, therefore, for the people to solve, is contained in the simple query : What is money ? An answer to this important inquiry will now be attempted to be given. Money is the product of law, and may be defined to be a legalized instrument or agent, created by the sovereign law of the State, and designed as a national medium for the exchange of products, or as legal fulfillment of a debt or obligation, created by contract or service rendered.

The power to make or coin money, is one of the most essential powers entrusted by the people to the Government.

The Constitution of the United States, Article I., Sec. VIII.—5. provides, that "the Congress shall have power to coin money, regulate the value thereof, and of foreign coin, and fix the standard of weights and measures," and in Article I., Sec. X.—1. It is further provided, "that no state shall coin money, emit bills of credit; make any thing else but gold and silver *coin* a tender in payment of debts."

From these constitutional provisions it will be seen, that the power to coin or make money is vested solely in Congress. The question to be considered is, how is this power to be legitimately exercised by Congress, and what material and what instrumentality is necessary to create or institute money ? A deep and wide spread opinion prevails among almost all classes of men, that some material of high intrinsic value is necessary for the institution of money. This opinion may go so far as to assert or claim that nothing but gold and silver are, or can be made money. But this idea is an exceedingly erroneous one, and it can be so easily demonstrated that it does not seem possible that any person who reasons can fail to perceive the error. This last assertion, of course, relates to the real or intrinsic qualities of money, considered as money, and has no reference to the mere abstract, hair-splitting, legal, or constitutional powers of government—these as used are only necessary to sustain the usurpations of financiers or to exclude the rights of the people. Taking it for granted then that the Government of the United

States, as it stands related to this question, like every civil government, has the sovereign power to institute money if it desires so to do, in any manner which shall be just and useful to the citizen and to the nation.

What attributes or powers are necessary for the institution of money, and how are they to be exercised?

First. There must be exercised or put forth the supreme or governmental power; and this must determine by law, denominations of value, of some easily appreciable, certain and definite amount. Weights and measures owe their efficiency to the same cause, and in the constitution are coupled with coinage, and fixing the value of money, and there is an appropriateness in the classification thus made, although it may be, and undoubtedly is true, that arising out of the theory of money, prevailing at that time, the idea was entertained that measures of value could be constructed by prescribing the quantity and quality of metal, which each coin should contain, which idea is wholly erroneous. And, further, it may also be true, that no accurate measure or designation of the value of property, labor, or use, ever has been, or can be constructed upon that principle; and as has been seen, money is not, accurately speaking, a legal standard of value, but a legal standard of payment. Yet, notwithstanding this, the subject matter of weights and measures as to quantities, and the fixing of scales, counters, or denominations of value, belong to this class of constitutional powers—both relate to the same class of objects, namely: the exact, just and accurate measurement and designation of property, and of all its uses as it stands related to quantity, quality and value. Now, in weights and measures, fixed and known quantities of property determined by law, from the least to the greatest amount, conveniently divided and designated by some general name, cognomen, or denomination, is essential to the idea of a measure. But when these denominations or measures are fixed definitely, and understood by the people, it is not essential that any particular object or material should be used to represent the idea, intended to be represented by the denomination used, other than the fitness of the article or material used for that purpose. In long measure, wood or some non-elastic, durable and light material is the best. Neither gutta-percha, gold, nor silver are essential. A golden yard stick would be much more expensive, not as durable, nor as easily used as wood. Wood, therefore, is the better material for yard sticks. The cloth measured by a golden yard stick, would not wear any longer, or be any more useful, than it would if measured by one made of wood. The same train of reasoning applies to liquid measures, and to weights. Besides, by not using either gold or silver in the manufacture of these measures, the owners of gold, or the world at large—at least all those who have to use gold are benefitted by having a more plentiful supply for useful and ornamental purposes.

Thus it is in relation to denominational measures, or more properly denominational designations of value. The attribute of value is in the property, labor, or use. A certain quantity and quality of property amount of service or labor, has a value which is determined by intrinsic properties or qualities, and by use. Now, money is merely a certain instrumentality, or agent, selected and appropriated by law, accurately to express the commercial value or use of the property, labor, or service.

This instrument, or agent, is purely a legal entity, and is instituted by making a denominational unit, which shall uniformly express some convenient, certain and appreciable amount of value in a certain piece of property, or in a certain kind of labor or service. For the accomplishment of this purpose, and for every desirable purpose in making an exchange, it makes no difference whether this denominational unit is a dollar, a crown, or a pound sterling, or whether the governmental power expressed, represented or designated by the unit be a pebble-stone, a notched stick, a clam shell, a piece of iron, copper, silver or gold. Its value as money is purely a *legal* value, and not an intrinsic one. It depends entirely upon its legal attributes. It is a legal certificate or mandate of the sovereign power of the state. It is in and of itself the product of the exercise of the highest power known in the civil state. Nothing less than the power thus exercised is competent to institute money. Its use, or office, when instituted, is that of an authentic or legalized counter or tally, and a public order for the amount named. For instance, A. has a horse worth a hundred dollars, he desires to put the horse into a wagon worth also a hundred dollars. B. wants the horse. is willing to pay a hundred dollars for him, but he has no wagon. B., therefore, pays the hundred dollars for the horse, and it is in a stick of a hundred notches or dollars, or in a greenback duly authenticated by the sovereign law. It is a legal certificate, that the holder has furnished that amount of property, or rendered that amount of service, and which entitles the holder to obtain from the government, or from any individual who desires to sell any property or service, which the holder desires to obtain, and is in the eye of the law a legal equivalent for such property or service to the amount, determined upon by the money. A., therefore, takes his notched stick or greenback, thus authenticated and made by the Government a legal tender, for all debts, public and private, and goes to C. who has wagons, and buys and pays C. a hundred dollars for his wagon. Who then will dispute the fact that this change or conversion of the horse into the wagon, is effected at a cheaper rate through this money medium than it could be by barter or by coin, and that the wagon and the horse, are each respectively worth as much, and will perform as much use after the change of ownership as before? Nay more. The horse and the wagon were perhaps in the hands of each of the original owners a surplus, which neither could profitably use. In this transaction on a miniature scale may be seen the law, and the appropriate use of money, in all the exchanges made in the world.

What then are the essential attributes of this money?

They are:

First—That it shall be instituted by the sovereign law of the state.

Second—That when instituted, it shall constitute a scale of equal parts sufficiently small to enable parties to transact with ease the least as well as the greatest amount of business.

Third—That this legal scale, counter, denomination, or tally, shall be stamped on paper, or some other durable material, having only an immaterial or nominal value.

Fourth—That this money when thus instituted, shall be a legal tender for all debts, public and private, and be exclusively the money of the nation. To these requisites there must be no exception. This, and this alone, would be money.

If, however, money as is claimed by some, derives its attributes from intrinsic worth, and that nothing but gold and silver are, or can be made money. Then legal enactments which go beyond the limit of determining the quantity and quality of the metal, will neither add to nor diminish its value, and such acts, therefore, if not vicious, are superrogatory, and for that reason, if for no other, should be omitted. If, on the other hand, it derives its efficiency entirely from legal enactments, then the substance or material of which money is made, should have, as has been before stated, only an immaterial, or legal value—otherwise, its legal attributes of value when arbitrarily mixed or compounded with intrinsic value, will make a compound which like gunpowder, if not as explosive and as destructive, will so combine, absorb and change its constituent elements and their value, that none but savans can determine what the real value of the compound is, or how it should be applied in determining other values.

Such indeed is now, and has been the result of all the moneys which have ever been instituted on such or a similar base. Under this system, of coinage laws, if they furnish a standard measure of value, or determine anything else than the weight and fineness of the metal, from whence comes the premiums and depreciation of coin? Are they from the standard measure coinage law, or from the intrinsic value of the coin, or are they the resultant effect of both causes? If aye; how much is attributable to the immutability of law, and how much to the intrinsic qualities of gold? Where is the golden *mean* which will enable the people to measure the values of their property? or in plain english: What is the measure of this standard measure with a premium on coin, ranging from one to twelve hundred per cent. above— or twenty per cent. below par? How are the people correctly to determine these questions, and of what use is a standard measure thus instituted? It serves the interests of the people by betraying their rights. Millions upon millions of dollars of property are taken out of the labor classes, by the increased demand for gold, and its metamorphosis, of coinage, gold bon l, impost, and gold tender laws beyond their power of supply. But, as this subject is examined at length, elsewhere, a reference has been made to it solely, for the purpose of showing that a standard measure of value cannot be made by connecting denominations of value indissolubly to gold or silver, or any other scarce commodity of high, intrinsic value, for the reason that value is an ever-changing property, dependent not only upon intrinsic qualities, but more largely upon legal and commercial uses, and that while the denominational value, does not, or cannot change, its commercial or market value does change to such an extent, as wholly to destroy the use of it, as a measure of value, but under all these financial laws, it is the most powerful agency, known, in misleading the people, and covering the wrongs inflicted upon them; and thus, that money should not rest or be built on any such changeable base. The remedy for these evils then lies in the direction indicated in the previous portions of this chapter, by the repeal of all coinage and other gold laws, and by the institution of money based upon the property of the people, and the sovereignty of the nation, and placed exclusively under governmental control. A redemption-money-system is merely a most odious, special, class-law-barter.

Whenever there shall be a money instituted and furnished by the Government, at cost, at convenient and reasonably accessible points, in manner, and amount, sufficient to enable every man who labors, or who has property to exchange, to transact his business with the facility it ought to be done; under such a law, even moderately well administered, there will be but few contractions or expansions of the money market, but such as arise from the increase or decrease of property and of exchanges. Such an event as a financial crash for the want of money or from its failure, would be unknown in the business vocabulary. It would be as impossible as the failure of a deed, mortgage, or bill of sale, a man, a horse, or steam engine, to perform the uses or objects designed or appropriate to the sphere of each. Bankers, brokers, and stock-jobbers, and the thieving created by them would also cease, and there could be inaugurated a form of society which nominally at least would approach a system of equity and fair dealing among men. An event which can never occur until coinage, banking, brokerage and public stocks shall be wiped out by law.

Coinage, as has been seen, furnishes a deceitful standard of value, and is the base of a fluctuating market, it is in fact a legal and potent instrumentality to derange markets, but never controls them but to the general injury of the producing and useful business classes.

For what use then are bonds payable in gold designed, or what good do they accomplish? They are simply a perpetual draft or drain upon the productive industry of a nation, to transfer arbitrarily, and directly the property from the men who earn it, to those who do not. Not only so, but they transfer it from those who would perform a real use, to those who are no real benefit to mankind, unless extortion, stealing and robbery, be deemed a benefit or use—gilded rights and squalid poverty mark their pathway. But ah! say these gentlemanly capitalists, the object of coinage is to furnish a standard measure of value.

When and where did such a standard practically exist? Its mythical character in premiums and depreciations of values has been shown, and there is no need to repeat the lesson taught. But then it is said, the object of bonds is to get money. The Government wants money to carry on all its varied operations, and its bonds, are issued as in the late terrible war, solely for this purpose. With an air of triumph it is frequently asked, how would the Government have carried on that war without the aid of the bonds, and capitalists? The answer to the query is: The Government wanted first—men, and *it* issued its mandate, and obtained them. It wanted money to pay for the services of the men, materials and munitions of war furnished, and it issued the *greenback*, and with it, paid for the services of the men, and for all the materials and munitions of war, which the country could furnish.

Why issue bonds to obtain money, when the Government was the only power which could create it? Why should the Government lease out to private individuals or to soulless corporations, at such exorbitant rates, its strongest and most essential power? Was it, that it might show its humility, by prostrating itself at the feet of the monster power it had created. Who was benefitted by this pusillanimous governmental conduct—the creator or creature?

Oh, yes! but then the Government was in great straits. It was obliged to obtain some articles and some munitions of war from foreign countries, and our money would not go there! What then was to be done? Exchange articles or commodities, when that failed, run in debt, and pay when we got the commodities with which to pay. Is not that what we did? Did we not obtain gold from the capitalists, and purchased the articles we wanted with gold? Not to any considerable extent. How could the capitalist of this or foreign countries have furnished the gold? The gold here has not at any one time much exceeded three hundred millions, and the gold and silver of the world does not much exceed, four or five billions, and our expenditures amounts in round numbers to some seven billions. How then could capitalists, taking into account the coin required elsewhere, have supplied the demand? It was not the gold then which capitalists furnished that enabled the Government to carry on the war, but it was merely staunch labor men, and the products of their **industry.**

But, did we not sell our bonds in Europe? Certainly, and at thirty and forty cents on the dollar, it is said ; at an enormous discount at least. Or, in other words, we through our bonds, sold them our commodities, at forty cents on the dollar, and purchased theirs at one hundred cents, and paid them, or are to pay them, six per cent. per annum, gold interest, for their gracious condescension in consenting to take our commodities at forty, and giving them in return one hundred. This is financier-ing, and the aid it furnished the nation.

What rendered such a terrible sacrifice necessary? A false monetary system, and a false business system based upon that money. Why should it be continued? What public good, or lawful private interest can be subserved by its continuance? None whatever. How is it sustained? There can be but one truthful answer given : It is because financiers demand it. These, through the politicians, and the political and commercial press, control public opinion, and by the vilest sophistry and lies, cover up the wrongs and robberies thus committed. Every intelligent and right minded man who examines the subject for himself, with any considerable degree of care, can easily perceive that this whole financial system is rotten from top to bottom. There is no soundness in it. It is useless to attempt to renovate it. Its origin in this country, and every other, is a brazen faced usurpa-tion of its sovereign power, and its longer continuance would be a solemn protest against the intelligence and integrity of the nation. The blindfold power of custom, and the inexhaustible resources of a new country may palliate the indifference of the past, but it can never be an apology for the continuance of this hateful, and unjust system.

CHAPTER IV.

A BILL FOR AN ACT

To ESTABLISH A UNIFORM CURRENCY, PROVIDE FOR THE MANAGEMENT AND LIQUIDATION OF THE NATIONAL DEBT AND FOR OTHER PURPOSES.

Be it enacted. &c., That the Secretary of the Treasury from the time this act shall take effect, is hereby authorized and required to issue Treasury certificates not bearing interest, in denominations of one, two, three, five, ten, twenty, fifty, one hundred, five hundred, and one thousand dollars; substantially, in the following form, signed by the Register of the Treasury, and by the Treasurer of the United States:

Twenty Dollars—Twenty Dollars—Twenty Dollars—Twenty Dollars—Twenty Dollars.
TWENTY DOLLARS **20** *Act of* .... *18* *No.* .... **20** TWENTY DOLLARS
TWENTY DOLLARS
B Lawful Money of the United States
Washington, ... *18* ......
Countersigned by
.... *Register of the Treasury.*
.... *Treasurer.*
Twenty Dollars—Twenty Dollars—Twenty Dollars—Twenty Dollars—Twenty Dollars.

Each of which certificates in addition to the above form, shall have their respective denominations of value printed on the margin, and appropriate vignettes on the face thereof, and such other numbers, marks, devices, and colors, as shall be best for the prevention of over issue, forging, or counterfeiting, and on the back thereof shall be printed the words: "Legal tender money certificate under Act of—(here inserting the date of this act)"—which certificate shall be received in payment, and shall be a legal tender in discharge of all debts, and demands now due, or which shall hereafter become due to, or payable by the United States, or to, or by any person or persons, corporation or corporations in the United States, except when the law under which the evidence of indebtedness of the United States arose, expressly requires or provides that the same shall be paid in coin.

Sec. 2. The Secretary of the Treasury is hereby authorized and required to issue bonds, signed in like manner as are the certificates mentioned in the first section of this act, and bearing date, on either the first day of January, April, July, or October of the year of their issue, in sums, or denominations not less than fifty dollars, nor more than ten thousand dollars, payable twenty years from the date thereof, each such bond other than those of fifty dollars, shall be for even hundred or hundreds of dollars, and each bond shall also bear interest at the rate of three per centum per annum, payable semi-annually, in certificates as per coupon thereto annexed. All of which bonds shall at any time be convertible at par, into the certificates mentioned in the first section of this act, and any holder of such bond, or bonds, may at any time so convert the same, as well before as after the lapse of five years from the date of such bond or bonds, the coupons being detached to their next day for the payment of interest. But all such bonds after the lapse of such five years may at any time be paid at par, by the United States with the aforesaid money, treasury-certificates, or other similar lawful money of the United States.

Sec. 3. The Secretary of the Treasury, is hereby required to pay all outstanding bonds or other obligations of the United States created since the first of July A. D. 1861, where the same shall become due and payable at the pleasure of the United States, in said treasury certificates, except as herein before excepted, or to give in exchange therefor if required by the owner, the aforesaid and hereby created bond or obligation of the United States, and if there shall not be raised coin sufficient to pay off the coin indebtedness of the United States, under excise and other laws now in force, then the Secretary of the Treasury is hereby authorized and required, to purchase with Treasury certificates, or with interest bearing bonds hereby created, by sealed bids, or otherwise, as may be most advantageous to the public interest, the coin necessary to pay off all the coin-interest, and principal bonds of the United States created under former laws, and the Secretary of the Treasury is hereby directed to give notice by publication in two newspapers, published in Washington city, to the holders of any such outstanding bonds or other obligations of the United States, to present the same at the Treasury-Department for such payment or exchange within ninety days from the date of such notice, or at the time the same may hereafter become due and payable, or redeemable at the pleasure of the Government, and the interest shall cease to accrue on all such bonds and other obligations of the United States not presented for such payment, or exchange within the time before mentioned, or from the time any such bond or obligation shall thereafter become due and payable, or redeemable at the pleasure of the Government.

Sec. 4. That the sixth and seventh sections of the act, "entitled an act to authorize the issue of the United States notes, and for the redemption or funding thereof, and for funding the floating debt of the United States," approved February 25th, A. D. 1862, as far as the same are applicable, shall apply to the Treasury certificates and interest bearing bonds hereby authorized to be issued, in like manner and effect as if the said sixth and seventh sections were herein incorporated, and the provisions and penalties of the sixth and seventh sections shall extend and apply to all persons who shall imitate, counterfeit, make, or sell any paper such as that used, or provided to be used, for the Treasury certificates, or bonds to be prepared in the Treasury buildings and to all officials of the Treasury Department engaged in engraving or preparing the Treasury certificates hereby authorized to be issued, and to all official and unofficial persons in any manner employed under the provisions of this act.

Sec. 5. *And be it further enacted,* That so much of the act entitled " An act to provide a national currency secured by a pledge of United States stocks, and to provide for the circulation and redemption thereof," approved February twenty-fifth, one thousand eight hundred and sixty-three, and so much of " An act to provide a national currency secured by a pledge of United States bonds, and to provide for the circulation and redemption thereof," approved June third, one thousand eight hundred and sixty-four, and also so much of all acts amendatory of either of the before mentioned acts as authorizes the Secretary of the Treasury, Comptroller of the Currency, or other officer or agent f the Government, to deliver circulating notes to any banking association, be, and the same are hereby, revoked and repealed.

SEC. 6. *And be it further enacted*, That it shall be the duty of he Secretary of the Treasury, and he is hereby directed to notify, within thirty days after the passage of this act, by publication or otherwise, all banking associations organized under the acts of which this act is amendatory, to return to the Treasury Department of the United States all circulating notes heretofore delivered to such associations, or any of them, upon pledge of United States stocks or bonds, within the six months after the passage of this act; and when any such association shall return ts circulating notes in sums of not less than one thousand dollars, it shall be the duty of the Secretary to deliver to such association a just proportion of the amount of the stocks or bonds deposited to secure the redemption of the circulating notes of such banking association: And wherever in any case such banking association shall neglect or fail to return to the Treasury Department the whole or any part of the circulating notes delivered to such association within six months from the passage of this act, then, and in every such case of neglect or failure, interest shall cease to accrue on all stocks or bonds deposited by any such association to secure the redemption of the circulating notes delivered to such association: But at all times whenever any such banking association shall neglect or fail to return to the Treasury Department the whole or any part of the circulating notes delivered to such association within two years from the passage of this act, then, and in every such case, it shall be the duty of the Secretary of the Treasury to declare the stocks or bonds remaining in the possession of the Government deposited by such association forfeited to the Government, and to redeem the outstanding notes of circulation of such association in the Treasury certificates authorized by this act.

SEC. 7. *And be it further enacted*, That it shall be unlawful for any banking association organized under either of said acts of which this act is amendatory, after six months from the passage of this act, to pay out or put in circulation any circulating medium or currency which is not made a legal tender and declared lawful money of the United States by act of Congress; and in case any such banking association shall violate the provisions of this section, it shall be the duty of the Secretary of the Treasury to declare the stocks or bonds remaining in the possession of the Government, deposited by such association, forfeited to the United States, and to redeem the outstanding notes of circulation of such association.

SEC. 8. *And be it further enacted*, That after ninety days from the passage of this act it shall not be lawful for the Secretary of the Treasury, or other disbursing officer or agent of the Government, to pay out the circulating notes of any banking association organized under the acts to which this is amendatory, or the United States legal tender notes heretofore issued; but shall discharge or pay all the bonded and other indebtedness of the United States, of every kind and nature incurred or contracted to be paid since the first day of July, eighteen hundred and sixty-one, or which may hereafter be incurred, in the Treasury certificates authorized to be issued and declared to be lawful money by this act, or to give in exchange for all such indebtedness the interest-bearing bonds authorized to be issued by this act, at the pleasure of the owner or holder of such indebtedness, (except where it has been by law expressly provided that payment shall be made in coin.)

SEC. 9. *And be it further enacted*, That it shall be the duty of the Secretary, or such other officer or officers as may be authorized by law, to keep a correct record of all the Treasury certificates and interest bearing bonds issued under or in pursuance of this act, describing the same by their numbers and denominations; also of all the bonds and other evidences of debt of the United States, and of the United States legal tender notes redeemed, and the circulating notes of banking associations returned to the Treasury Department, describing the same in like manner, and publish monthly reports showing the amount of Treasury certificates and interest-bearing bonds issued, and the amount of bonds and other evidences of debt, and United States legal-tender notes redeemed, and of the circulating notes of banking associations returned to the Treasury Department; and shall cancel and destroy all such bonds or other evidences of debt, and United States legal-tender notes so redeemed, and circulating notes of banking associations so withdrawn from circulation, and shall make annual reports thereof to Congress, as now is, or hereafter may be provided by law: *Provided*, That the Treasury certificates and bonds authorized to be issued by this act shall not be so destroyed unless they shall be mutilated or rendered unfit for use.

The passage of the foregoing bill would be an attempt to establish a just system of finance, a re-investment of the long usurped sovereign power hitherto leased out and held by financiers and bankers for unlawful gain. It would, therefore, be necessary to prohibit these classes under severe penalties from issuing any bank or other paper designed for a circulating medium, or from in any way interfering with the circulation of the money issued under said act, either by unlawfully withdrawing from circulation a large amount of said notes, or in any other manner or by other unlawful device to attempt to depreciate the value and the usefulness of the legal money. It might also be necessary further to provide, temporarily at least, to issue money to a certain limited extent, secured by a pledge or lien upon property, both personal and real, or by State stocks. Under certain clearly defined limits to provide for every possible contingency which might arise in carrying into effect the Act establishing the people's money in place of bankers faithless promises.

The Government cannot well be too provident in making provisions to furnish an ample supply of money, and on the other hand it cannot be too cautious in guarding against every form of abuse, which would be likely to arise in this exercise of the sovereign power. The ideas, habits and customs of the people formed under the usurped reign of financiers, might possibly be used to retard the inauguration and practical working of the new system. Financiers and bankers will unquestionably throw every obstacle in the way, which is calculated to defeat the just objects intended by this Act. Nothing less than war could have inaugurated the reign of the "greenback," and have laid the foundation for the establishment of a just system. The great mistake made in the first place was in not relying upon the "greenback" entirely for our home supply of products and materials, and only borrowed money to procure what was absolutely necessary to be obtained from foreign countries.

The only effectual and safe remedy for the financial evils we now suffer, and which will be indefinitely increased under our past and present regime, is at once to abolish national banking, our gold interest bond, to pay those where the whole is payable in coin, and to return immediately and unconditionally to the people's money, made a legal tender for all debts public and private without exception. We shall thus inaugurate a just system, and redeem our country from a slavery of money so enormous and so terrible that even African slavery, is a mere shadow, compared with this bond-representative-money-interest-eating out system. Let any man who has examined this subject carefully, deny if he can, that African slavery, bad as it might be, was anything more than a mere pigmy in enormity by the side of this cold-blooded or heartless device. If such was its character in the past, what must it not be that is evil in the future. To get rid of it, and to establish a just system the people may count the privations and cost of war a trifling sacrifice to obtain such a permanent good.

The benefits of instituting money in the manner proposed, may be summed up as follows: A legalized instrument of payment furnished by the Government, is substituted for a mere promise to pay; its power is the sovereignty of the people; its base their property; its amount depends upon the public will, and not that of the financiers. They furnish the property, and determine for themselves how much they will put into money, and how much into lands, goods, wares and merchandize. A property base is furnished instead of a credit base, and sovereign law controls the circulation instead of the interest of the speculating sovereign bankers. Thus, the money power is detached from a species of property, to be attached to all property. If then A., B. C. and D. choose to buy and import 300,000,000 of dollars worth of foreign goods, more than we have other commodities for which to exchange, they can buy their gold if they choose, to fill the foreign demand, and the exchange of the people's products can be made through the medium of their legal, honest money, and no derangements of business or industry will take place, except perhaps among those who needed this gold and silver to make nose and ear-rings or some other equally useless purpose. Now, do the people through just laws want this money within their reach, at cost, or do they want it upon the terms fixed by bankers, and through laws framed to build them up at their expense? If they desire the former, then the act proposed will meet their approval, if the latter, they have only to continue the convertible gold base, and gold interest bond schemes of the capitalist. We have thus distinctly presented some of the leading points involved in this issue between the people's money and the banker's "*currency*,"

. ̦ ᴜᴘᴏꜱᴇ of provoking honest, earnest enquiry into this important subject—on the part of the people themselves.

But here we are met with the objection that governmental systems have ever proved a failure. While this is true as applied to certain governmental issues, it is also true that all systems based upon gold and silver, have ever proved failures of gigantic proportions. Nevertheless we are repeatedly told, that all that is necessary now to remove our deranged finances, and to restore confidence, is to fund the greenback, and inaugurate specie payments. All these representations may be, and undoubtedly are, very satisfactory to those who make unjust gain through such fraudulent means ; but their gold base is as false and as baseless as dreams and visions of the night. Neither in this country, nor in England has a specie basis lasted for a period exceeding fifteen years, and seldom has it lasted ten. In 1844, the English Government made five pounds the smallest denomination of notes, which the Bank could issue, erroneously imagining, that these commercial disasters result from an excessive issue of paper instead of an excessive purchase of goods and wares very much beyond the products furnished in exchange for their purchase. But there has been no less than three most severe financial revulsions since the passage of that Act, and indeed it ought to tinge the check of any man, with a blush of shame, who has been familiar with the bitter history of finance for the last fifty years, to even intimate that there is any reliability to be placed upon any money or currency, based on what is called a specie basis.

Yet, while these ill-omened prophets on governmental paper issues can see nothing but stability and value in their own system, they do not fail to remind us of the fatal misfortunes which have usually overtaken " all the Government paper issues ever made." They do fail to give us another fact, equally important to be known, and that is, that these governmental paper issues which have proved so fatal to the interest of the people and so discreditable to the financial wisdom of Governments who instituted them, were in no sense, either in substance or form, money, or if they were, they originated out of, and were inseparably connected with the false system which these financiers so loudly commend. Another omission equally unfortunate for the truth of their representations is, that those paper issues which have been money — have been generally good, and some of them for centuries have borne a premium over coin, averaging over twenty per cent.

Although not much can be expected from the despotic governments of the old world which is calculated to benefit the people, and much less, as a general rule, ought we to copy after them. Yet, two important questions relating to money may be considered as settled, adverse to the gold base theories of financiers, if any thing can be settled under such grossly partial class laws. The first is, that State paper money, when the debt itself is circulated has been universally good, and the second is, that the only reliable fund for the present redemption of a paper money has not been gold or silver, but the avails of the property purchased by the paper or currency.

In the ensuing chapters the history of money bearing upon these two questions will be examined at length for the purpose of showing that the system of Treasury certificates is not a mere theory, like the Financiers system, but a theory based upon fundamental principles, nnd well established facts. The lessons taught by the Banks of Venice, Genoa, Amsterdam and Hamburg can be studied with profit by statesmen and people. The history of these banks, therefore, will be next presented.

CHAPTER V.

THE BANK OF VENICE—ITS HISTORY.

The Bank of Venice was established in 1171. It owes its origin to a forced loan taken from the most wealthy Venetians to sustain the Republic in a war against the Grecian Emperor, Manuel, at the same time carrying on a war with the Emperor of the East. Each citizen was required to contribute according to his ability, and by a decree of the Great Council, the office of Chamber of Loans, (*La Camera Degl. Imprestiti*) was instituted. The contributors to the loans were made creditors to that office, and were to receive an annual interest of four per cent. "This was no doubt far below the customary charge of that day; but whether foreseen or not, the privileges of the *Chamber of Loans* soon indemnified these public creditors for this then low rate of interest." Colwell, p. 289.

These loans were inscribed in a book, authenticated and made evidence of the whole debt, as well as what belonged to each subscriber. This interest was punctually paid into the office, and thence distributed to each creditor. This practice in the course of time exhibited to all the lenders how simple and easy to pay and receive debts among themselves by transfer on these books; and from the moment that the advantages which commerce might derive from this method of paying debts was perceived, bank money was invented. Econ Politique, par Henri Storch; Vol. IV. p. 95.

Facility of transfer, coupled with the security of the State, and regular payment of the interest, seems to have led to a very rapid circulation of this loan. Colwell, p. 289. There was at Venice that which more than any previous commercial policy, opened men's eyes to an advantage of great importance, contributing alike to the prosperity of the State, and to the benefit of trade. She was the glorious inventress of the Guarrantied Bank, (*banco garantito*) differing both in its operations and by its security from common banks, as much as from those called public banks. Broggia Tratte delle Moneti Vol. II. p. 270. It is worthy of remark, says Colwell, that this very efficient mode of adjustment discovered and used so largely at this early period in the history of commerce, was not dependent for its efficacy on the guarantee of the Republic. That guarantee sprung out of the mode in which the bank originated; this convenient mode of liquidation came from the use of the new substitute for money.

"The facility of payment furnished by the bank, which made it the admiration of Europe, honorable at once to the Government and merchants of Venice, and a support to the pride and power of its people, consisted in substituting as a medium of payment the DEBT of the REPUBLIC for CURRENT COIN."

"This system of payments, without the use of coin, was so well adapted to the exigencies of commerce, that it was maintained in its full vigor, in the great commercial city of Venice, for almost five hundred years. It was an institution or device of the credit system, for by its aid payments were effected, and that to a vast amount annually, without any use of coins or bullion." It only perished when the city itself fell, at the conquest of Italy by Napoleon; but the conqueror carried off no coin, no penny of prey. The credits of the bank were crushed under the rude touch of an invading foe; they were lost to the proprietor, but no equivalent passed into the hands of the destroyers. If the holders of these credits suffered, the invaders were not enriched. In assuming the sovereignty of Venice, the conqueror assumed the right and the duty of making good these bank credits."

In the course of time it was found convenient to have a place of deposit for specie and bullion, and the Government established a department for that purpose, as a co-ordinate branch of the bank. This was simply a place of deposit, and was in no way connected with the operations of the other departments of the bank, except as to its management, being under governmental control each branch having its own peculiar mode of management, governed by the specific objects for which it was instituted. The necessity which existed of making occasional payments in gold, or coin, gave rise to the opening of this deposit office, for those who wished to be paid in coin. "Experience proved that this measure did not cause any sensible diminution in the funds, (the paper, credit, or money,) of the bank."

Dict. de Com. par Savary, article Banque, p. 276. The Government acting in the capacity of a depository, performed that duty, by effecting a change of the ownership of the coin deposited to any extent desired by the owner. It exercised no discretion, simply followed the rules laid down for the Government of the transfer of deposits.

The amount thus deposited fluctuated largely, but the surplus of coin not used was always very large. The Government in times of pressing need used this deposit.

The deposit or cash office suspended payments twice, once for several years. Yet the management of the older branch had been so satisfactory, that the transfers of these removed deposits continued as if the specie was present. The Government received them in payment, and the two departments of the bank, practically, during the suspension were resolved into one. Each fund being equally and simply a public debt, but the old bank credits maintained their higher rate of premium over that of the specie debt. A writer in the London Encyclopedia not understanding this fact, has exhibited the premium on the bank fund as a depreciation, he says, " that derangements in the social economy of the state soon ensued, the agio or difference between the current money and transferable amounts at the bank attained to thirty per cent." But unfortunately for Encyclopediast, the agio instead of being against the bank, was in its favor, and against the specie credit. Its funds bore thirty per cent. premium over current coin, and remained near this high rate until the Government fixed the premium at twenty per cent., where it remained so long as the bank existed. This agio was clearly not understood by Encyclopediast, who was probably a British gold worshipper, and he could not conceive of any good reason why paper should for centuries bear a premium over gold, and therefore, he quoted the agio or premium as a depreciation. But, nevertheless, the Government bank paper did bear this high premium for centuries, and the reason probably was, that although there was no coin in the bank, its credits were the funds in which payments were made. If these credits had been convertible into coin, at will, the agio would never have existed, for the reason, that the moment the holders of credits advanced the price, specie if it had been a legal tender would have been the medium of payment.

The full operation of this bank credit is so well explained in a work entitled: Parfait Negociant, Vol. I. page 463, that we give the article entire.

"If Jean, Pierrre, Claude and Jacques, and consequently every inhabitant of the same town, had but one banker, who kept an account with each one of them, in a register provided for that purpose; this banker could make all their reciprocal payments without moving a cent of their money, and it would suffice simply to write upon his register the receipt from one, and the payment by another from which would result two things— they would avoid the trouble of receiving and counting money, and the expense of each having a cashier and bookkeeper."

"Another respect in which the position of this banker would be advantageous to them would be, that he could put the money of all to good use, without diverting it from its proper destination, or interrupting the progress of their payments which would be effected there by means of his books, and a third advantage would arise, if this same banker would lend the money thus economized to his customers by which they would augment their trade, both at home and abroad."

"This is what the Republic of Venice happily accomplished by the establishment of its bank, which became a perpetual bank for its inhabitants. It received from them money previously employed in payment of merchandize in gross, and of bills of exchange, and gave them the Government paper, credit, or power for it, and by public edict all payments for merchandize, in gross, were to be made only in bank. All debtors were obliged for this purpose to carry their money to the bank, and receive credit therefor, and all creditors to receive payment there. Every payment was made by a simple transfer of a credit upon the books of the bank from one to another. He, who was a creditor upon the book of the bank became debtor as soon as he assigned to another, who thus became a creditor in his place; and so on, from one to another, the parties simply changing their position of debtor and creditor; without any necessity of a payment in money." This self-same result can be better attained through the medium of the treasury certificate.

The lesson then, taught by the Bank of Venice, is worthy serious consideration of the Government and people of the United States. Way back in the twelfth century is a governmental paper money, not based on gold, nor payable in coin or bullion, which by being made a legal tender for all taxes and dues to government and people at only four per cent. interest, promptly paid, is not only worth more than coin-certificates of deposits, but bearing from twenty to thirty per cent. premium over coin and bullion for a period of five hundred years. What a contrast between that paper money, and the United States gold bonds and money. Here is a nation with annual revenues for a series of years, amounting to between four and five hundred millions of dollars, with the most fertile soil, unbounded resources, and the most intelligent and active population in the world. Yet her paper, bearing six per cent. gold interest, payable semi-annually, is mere trash in the hands of the gold speculators and gambling stock jobbers to be hawked about in every market of the world, at thirty per cent. discount.

What are our statesmen doing to remedy the evil, and remove this national stigma. We answer conciliating kings, courts, and capitalists — our foreign ministers are interesting European aristocrats with high wrought eulogies on the greatness of the model Republic, and the grandeur of her overshadowing power, and by graciously assuring them that we are following in their wake.

The toiling millions toil day and night, and count well their scanty supplies to meet their largely increased burthens. While statesmen at home ignoring alike the great lessons of history and the sober dictates of common sense, are groping their dark way through the mazes of English financiering, vainly trying to find the specific gravity of a gold base. Thus its annual accumulation of over four hundred million dollars of revenue, instead of being used in a way to aid the productive industry of the country in developing its resources, schemes are devised to aid the capitalist through a gold bond and specie laws, to control the price of labor and its products—thus to convert their paper currency which they have furnished the Government into gold, and to make the people pay an annual gold interest until this conversion into gold actually takes place.

But we here venture to remind these gold theorist statesmen and financiers also, that there are other objects, and other commodities too, more essential to the welfare of the nation than gold, and the day will come, when the people will discover, that all these gold bond, and gold base theories, mean a perpetual robbery of them, for the benefit of the capitalist, without any corresponding benefit to the people themselves. We venture further to remind them, that if the Government of Venice could devise a plan by which the government debt, at four per cent., could for five hundred years be made a medium of exchange bearing a premium of over twenty per cent. during that whole period—it does not speak well for the intelligence and virtue, of statesmen and savans, living in the full blaze of the light, intelligence, improvement and christian virtue of the nineteenth century, to have the debt of the greatest, most enterprising and intelligent nation in the world at thirty per cent. discount—even though these statesmen and savans succeed in settling the important preliminaries of proving the specific gravity of a gold base to the bottom.

We, therefore, offer for their serious consideration a system, that will reduce the cost of a circulating medium to three per cent., destroy a discount of thirty per cent., and if there is to be a premium of twenty per cent. like that of the ·Venetian debt, have shown them the reason for it, and we kindly ask them to save that premium for the benefit of the people.

CHAPTER VI.

BANK OF GENOA—HOUSE OF ST. GEORGE.

The Genoese system of finance was one of the most complicated and extraordinary of which history gives any account. For ages, the nobles of Genoa kept the state in a continual ferment almost amounting to civil war. Out of this troublous condition originated its financial system. Its history is principally useful for the purpose of illustrating the fact: First, that paper money has from the first dawn of civilization been far more effective as a medium of exchange than coin, second that the origin of banking is an usurpation of the sovereign power which ought not, and will not be longer tolerated by a people who are free and independent.

It has been shown that the Bank of Venice had its origin in a forced loan, and that the public debt thus created was made the principal medium of exchange at four per cent. interest, and bearing a premium for five centuries, averaging over twenty per cent. over coin—that the debt was kept at that amount, which preserved its value, while it furnished a reliable currency for all the purposes of trade. The Government without any pledges of gold or silver, or of any other guaranties, except an evidence of the debt entered upon the books of the bank, and enforced by a legal tender Act, were enabled to give the people a currency far more valuable than either gold or silver. This presents a strong contrast not only with the Bank of Genoa, but in this particular with all the great banks of modern date which instead of improving in matter of justice to the people have like the Bank of Genoa largely increased their power.

The Genoese capitalists, too, like those of more modern date had no faith in the credit of the State, only so far as they could extort the utmost securities and strongest guarrantees which the Government could give. This line of policy was strictly pursued on the part of the public creditors for more than a century, and by a continued amendment of laws and concession of rights, these Shylocks like our modern ones, obtained not only their pound of flesh with the living, gushing blood, oozing at every pore, but they became the essential government, having their own magistrates, privileges entirely independent of the State. The supreme power was so far in their hands that in the violent party strifes, bloodshed and civil war which was continually occurring, they held their undivided and unimpaired sway over the people. They had no occasion to look after the payment of their interest by the government; they had already secured every loan by an assignment of taxes, customs, or other revenues, sufficient to pay all interest. It does not appear, however, that they had then learned the genteel art of exchanging their irredeemable promises to pay, with the government, and then to extort from the government without law or right the payment of principal and interest in gold. Neither does it appear that they had learned the more convenient mode of making the government collect, and stand expenses and losses. Their assignment of the public revenue was intended to be amply sufficient to pay the interest, and the creditors took the trouble, cost and loss of collections on themselves.

In 1302 a reconstruction of the Genoese financial system took place, and the public income, or the creditors of the government were organized into a public body, having among others the following officers:

1. Four VISITORS, two nobles and two of the people, who must be over thirty years of age with estates not less than 300 lires, and not in debt to the state. They were sworn to fulfil its duties and held their office six months; they were aided by four clerks. All other officers had to make to them an annual report of payments and balances, and their oaths of office were filed with these visitors. Their documents were required to be under seal (the face of St. Michael).

2. Two CONSOLS who had charge of transfers of shares and other duties, two other officers were afterwards added, called comforters (comfortators). In 1321, four councillors were added, the whole constituting the Council of Transfer.

3. KEY-KEEPERS, (Clavigeri,) they had charge of the money, and made all payments.

4. The JUDGE, (delGuidici del capitolo,) who had jurisdiction of all questions touching the collection of the public revenue, by the public creditors.

5. The VICARIO, was a judge, having criminal as well as civil jurisdiction, in matters of revenue, taxes, fines, etc.

6. Twenty of the largest foreign creditors might at a special meeting select from their number a Judge, (Guidice de Calleghe) who held a special office, when sitting as a Court, he was to call to his assistance other creditors who could vote with him. Securities for debt, or for good behavior of officers was first to be approved by this Judge, and no nobles could be security.

7. FARMERS of the revenue, (Appaltatori.) An extensive system for subletting the collections of the taxes, revenues, etc. All the contracts and acts of these *Farmers* constituted a large portion of the business of the judges above named.

8. PROTECTORS. These had charge of seeing that the revenue laws were faithfully executed.

This shows where the idea of creating a complicated mode of assessing, and collecting government subsidies originated—having farmed the people out to capitalists, it became necessary to have a large number of officers to enforce the collection of these dues from the people, one class to steal, and the other to watch them while doing it. The ingenious device of making the people do this collecting through the government directly, had not then been discovered.

In the early part of the fifteenth century the murmurs of the people, finally, compelled the government to appoint a commission composed of eight persons, to furnish a plan of reform—the appointment of these commissioners was made in 1407. They found that these various bodies of *compere*, or public creditors, each holding their own special class of securities, had as might have been expected when the state was let out to capitalists, involved the whole subject in an injurious complication. The commissioners determined upon paying off the public debt, and having the grants and securities resumed by the State. In other words they brought forward a new funding and banking scheme. Shares of 100 lires each, in amount sufficient to pay the whole debt was proposed to be issued, and the banking House of St. George was to be established—the state to re-assign to this bank such portions of the public revenues as were deemed an adequate security, and upon the same terms, and with the same rights, privileges and remedies, formerly enjoyed by the Compere.

In pursuance of this recommendation of the commissioners, the

Bank of St. George was established, and the interest on the public debt reduced from eight to seven per cent. under the control of the state.

The people appeared to be well satisfied with the change, but they soon found they had only changed masters. The Bank had not only the same power, and was as watchful as the Compere had been, but they obtained during that century nine further concessions, and among these was an exemption of bank shares and deposits from attachment and confiscation for either public, or private claims.

The Government of the Bank consisted of the following officers:

1. A GENERAL COUNCIL of 480 members, holders of not less than ten shares, and to be over 18 years of age.

2. Eight PROTECTORS, six of whom over thirty, and two over twenty years of age, holders of 11 shares.

3. Thirty-two ELECTORS, who selected the Protectors.

4. PROVEDITORS, who had served as Protectors.

5. Eight PROCURATORS, six over thirty, and two over twenty-five years of age—holders of 40 shares.

6. The COUNCIL of 1444, consisted of eight members qualified as the Procurators.

7. Eight COUNCILLORS of the Salt Import, with the same qualification.

8. Four SINDICATORS, holders of 40 shares—two to be twenty-five, and two to be over twenty-two years of age.

9. The TREASURER-GENERAL, elective by the Protectors and Council of 1444. He gave a security 90,000 lires, and a deposit of 160. He was to be over thirty years of age—not engaged in any other business, have no interest in St. George, or any bank, or any concern of bankers, or other dealing in money. He held his office five years, subject to annual confirmation, but was not allowed to have even an account current with any officer of the bank. He could only secure and pay coins from the mints of Genoa, Spain, Venice, Florence and Naples, at the weight and price fixed by the Protectors. Other money was taken by government tariff. Bigletti for dividends, were payable in Scudi, at 4.10 lires. Cartulario, or bills for deposit, were payable in the same coin received. All false money was to be cut. The Treasury was never to be without the sum of 24,000 lires- The Treasurer kept one of the three keys of

the Treasury, the Prior another, and the Sindaco of the Compere the third.

The salary of the Treasurer-General was at first 1,660 lires, but was afterwards raised to 3,256, and an increased deposit was required.

There were a host of subaltern officers such as Revisors, Fiscal Advocates, Judges, Chancellors, Consultors, etc., to all whom special duties were assigned, similar to those above named, and too numerous to be here given.

In 1539, a severe famine occurred, when the government in order to give employment to the poor, obtained aid from the House of St. George, and this occasioned a new contract with the Republic, whereby the taxes, and customs, previously pledged to the bank, were mostly fully conveyed to it. And it was further stipulated by the Republic, that no new taxes should be levied which would in any way affect those assigned to the Bank, without its consent. The Doge, the Governors and their successors, at the instance of the Bank officers were every year required to swear upon the Holy Evangelists to observe all the conditions, covenants, and stipulations of this new contract, and the Bank was required to pay into the public Treasury 50,000 lires per annum.

Upon assistance rendered the government in an extraordinary public emergency, three annual payments of interest were postponed each, three years. The first being payable on the fourth, the second on the fifth, and the third on the sixth year. The Bank then opened a new account with the shareholders of these deferred dividends; and each dividend was credited to them in the order stated above. The bank received them for all taxes, and dues, deducting interest for the time they had to run to maturity. In this way these deferred dividends became as saleable as bank shares, the shareholders losing only the interest, while they gained a credit for three years income. Thus these deferred dividends were turned into money, as occasion required, by deducting the interest.

The ecclesiastical share-holders, acting mostly as trustees, pretended they could not give their assent without violating their consciences, but Pope Calistus III., pope-like, at the instance of the Bank, granted the dispensation of delay asked for, which was a full salvo for their consciences.

This three-year deferred dividend-system, was afterwards

repeated, and Pope Sixtus IV., granted a like dispensation in favor of the bank, to the full satisfaction of the ecclesiastics, this was in 1749.

These deferred dividends, owing to the manner in which the Bank permitted them to be used, as above explained, were in great demand in making purchases and payments. They were denominated Paghe Scritti, or Lire de Paghe, they were used as collaterals upon terms fixed every year in advance, generally at twenty-five per cent. discount.

Previous to the year 1673, the bank shares had been largely employed in purchases and payments as a substitute for money. And deposits had been received, and bills issued for them to suit the depositor. Its commercial agency, however, had not been very extensive, but the diverse coinage of Europe, Asia and Africa, which had been flowing into the city for a considerable period of time, required a remedy. The officers of the bank, therefore, made an application to the Government for an enlargement of the privileges and powers of the bank, and it was granted.

Bills of exchange payable in Genoa of any amount, with all other debts over 100 lires were made payable at the bank, and these provisions were enforced by heavy penalties. From this time the transfers of shares and deposits assumed the simple and easy process observed at the Bank of Venice.

The Bank under this Act increased its business so rapidly, that it was deemed advisable by its officers to divide its customers alphabetically into four divisions, with separate organizations of officers, clerks, books, etc., but these departments, though independent of each other, were integral parts of the institution as a whole.

The accounts of gold and silver received, were kept in separate books. There were also three separate treasuries: one for coin to be returned on demand in the very coin deposited; one a general repository for bank and silver coin at bank rates, and another for current coins at rates fixed by the government, and tables of which were furnished the Bank.

The bank shares, into which the public debt was divided were called "luoghi," (places) being 100 lires each. The lire had a similar origin in Italy with the livre in France and the pound in England *i. e.* a weight. Coins of this denomination are still in use in Milan, and Genoa, worth about fourteen cents; what it was worth anciently is not easy of ascertainment. It is probable that its value was much greater than at present.

These "luogho" or shares were transferable verbally, in the presence of a bank notary, by writing, by will, or by mortgage. They were extensively used in commerce in making purchases and payments. For more than two centuries they were considerable above par.

Carlo Cuneo, has furnished a table of the rates of dividends taken from the books of the bank from the year 1409 up to 1800, and of the price of shares from 1559 down to the same period of time. In 1559, shares were at 48; in 1582, at 112; in 1606, 219; 1621, at 278. The fluctuations occasioned by this advance were frequent, and very great, varying from 140 to 200, down to 1739.

The quotations afterwards are in scudi, of 4 lires 4.20 In 1740, they were quoted at 30 scudi, over 25 per cent. above par. This fluctuation of price continued down to 1797, between 20 and 34 scudi; in 1798, at 8; in 1800, at 4.

The deferred dividends (valute delle paghe) from 1559 to 1764, bore a very steady price, and were therefore much employed as a currency, or money.

The currencies of Genoa were :

1. Bank shares of the public debt, 100 lires each. This was circulated as freely as bank deposits, and it was the base of a money of account fixed at a point about twenty-five per cent. above par, in which these bank shares were afterwards expressed. The common currency was then about twenty-five per cent. below this Bank money, (valutæ banco.)

The money of account, called bank money, never varied. It was a reliable register of values, of coins, bank shares, and other currencies. The bank also issued bills, in the denominations of this money of account, which passed as a currency the same as the bank shares.

2. Bank deposits were largely employed as a currency, bank bills for deposits were also used, and both deposits and bills represented coins of full weight and value, payable on demand in coin, but the coins were only used as merchandize, not as coin.

3. The deferred dividends of the bank, constituted another currency much used. This was subject to a deduction of interest, and such fluctuations as the market imposed. In 1559, it was

14 lires, 4 s., during the century they rose to 17, for another century they stood at 18 lires.

4. The currency for retail and common business, was called the fuori banco, or out-of bank moneys; it was composed of coin worn out, clipt, pared, sweated and plugged. This coin was taken by the common people (as is generally the case, if anybody is to be cheated it is them) at its nominal or denominational value, without regard to actual value. This *base* money formed a money of account, much used, among the common people, in all their small dealings; but did not extend to the larger transactions of commerce.

The Bank of Venice circulated the debt of the Republic, and the ownership of coins—the former at a more uniform rate—for a longer period of time, and above par than any money, which has ever been issned. But the Bank of Genoa issued both classes as money, and it also issued the first bank bills ever put into circulation. These bills, however, were not in any certain fixed denominations as now used, but were for such amounts as the parties desired.

The holder of government securities, or coin, deposited either, or both with the Bank, and took a bill for the amount which took rank in value, according to the character of the deposit; government securities, however, almost uniformly rated higher than coin.

The Bank of St. George was inferior in commercial importance to the Bank of Venice; it had much larger guarrantees, or in other words, it took an actual security from the government, in the form of a pledge of revenues for the performance or payment of its contract, or obligation.

It had also the advantage of having a higher rate of interest; and of receiving enough out of the revenues assigned to pay amply for the cost of collection—yet it never attained anything like the amount of circulation; nor the uniformity of value, that the Bank of Venice did. It however held a high position in the commerce of Europe for some two centuries; and has been more largely copied in the bank legislation and commercial regulations in the European nations, than any institution of those early ages of the world.

The reason for this preference, was not on account of its superior advantages as an agent of commercial exchange, but on account of its superior advantages as an instrument of power.

The issue of interest securities, and of money or currency bearing interest, gives a double income, and is a more effective instrument of deranging values, and reaping the advantages of that derangement than any device yet invented.

But we shall have occasion to examine into this subject more in detail, when we come to treat of the Bank of England. In that institution is concentrated all the labor-robbing, and nobility-class-sustaining despotic powers which have been contained in all the institutions which have preceded it.

There is, however, one point in the institution of the Bank of Genoa to which the attention of the reader is especially directed, and that is to the extension of the powers of the bank to issue bills of credit, and to make them payable at the Bank.

The Bank never attained any particular celebrity, until the passage of that Act. It was not specie in the bank, nor in the hands of the people, but it was the getting rid of the necessity of using coin in payments, which gave to the paper of the Banks of Venice and Genoa, both a greater efficiency than ever was, or could be attained by coin as a medium of exchange.

From the period that the Bank of Genoa was put on a par with the Bank of Venice as to issuing its bills, and making payment in them at the Bank; its advancement in business was so great, that it had to be divided into four departments to accommodate the business public.

Its immense amount of circulation and its success is attributable to that cause, and thus to a legal efficiency, or governmental regulation, and not to a coin base.

CHAPTER VII.

THE BANK OF AMSTERDAM.

This institution furnishes a paper issue of a somewhat anomalous character under governmental management and control. It was a heavy, bungling device of credit, yet it was so much better managed, and so much more useful than the average range of modern banks that its history is worthy of more than a passing notice.

It was instituted in 1609. The Bank of Venice had been established so many centuries before, that it is surprising that the magistrates of Amsterdam with such an exemplar should have constructed so clumsy and so expensive a system. The probabilities, however, are that the people of Amsterdam had been so long under the gold and silver enslaving system, and became so wedded to it by custom, that they had come to think that there was but little of value in the world worth possessing, except these metals.

Though it seems that the multiplicity and bad character of the coin, its wear by use; with the counterfeiting, plugging, gutting and sweating, aided somewhat perhaps by the dangers and difficulties of keeping and transporting, on account of dishonest agents, robberies and pirates, reconciled the burghers to the idea of dispensing with the use of the golden idol, and was what led to the institution of the Bank of Amsterdam as a safe repository, or *dead-pledge*, (mortuum vadium) of their precious idol.

This Bank was virtually and simply a depository. The deposit was not to be withdrawn, but kept—while the ownership of the coin, or bullion, was to be circulated in its place.

The transfer of the ownership of the coin was so far a coin deal, but inasmuch as the order passed the title, but not the coin itself; it was to that extent purely a credit transaction. The coin upon which this order was drawn, had been previously taken to the Bank, scrutinized, tested, valued, and credited to the depositor. At this time, these coins and bills of exchange, coin-payable, were at from eight to ten per cent. discount in the City of Amsterdam. The government of the city and of its magistrates was the security given to the public for the integrity of the Bank. The provision making all bills of exchange over 600 florins payable in bank, gave it its rapid and permanent establishment, as it had before done in the case of the Banks of Venice and Genoa. This at once concentrated payments at this point; and compelled every person who had bills to pay, to deposit his coin or bullion, and to open an account with the Bank. The depositor was charged by the bank five per cent. for discount on his coin or bullion; and was subject to a charge of ten florins for opening the account. But the bank money soon bore a premium, which amply compensated for the expense of opening an account, and for the loss or discount.

The depositor having opened his account, was then prepared to make his payments by a transfer of the part or a whole of his title to the deposit; but he was permitted to make only one transfer a day.

To receive, keep, and pay by means of the transfer of the title constituted the business of the bank, this was effected thus:

Folio 1609.

Messrs. Commissioners of the Bank, please pay to John Smith, the sum of one thousand florins, four sols, and six deniers.

Amsterdam, 25. June, 1709.   Peter Smith.

F. 1000 4s. 6d.

The drawee, or his special agent, on presentation was entitled to a credit, and the drawer was charged. Deposits in the hands of all holders were exempt from seizure by attachment, or other legal process, but the fund itself remained here locked up forever.

In January and July, each year, for fifteen days the bank was closed, books balanced, and a new account opened. Depositors books were at the same time compared with the bank entries, to determine the correctness of the bank accounts. For three days following the opening of the bank, parties could transfer at pleasure the amounts by them received. Banking hours were from 7 A. M. to 3 P. M. After 11 A. M. transfers cost six sols, before that hour two. The bank-book-folio, in which the account was kept, was numbered on the order or check. Accounts numbered from one, upward, and the folio was made to correspond. Each clerk had only a specified number of these accounts, when the check was presented the clerk in charge readily turned to the page, and made the proper transfer.

This mode of payment, as the deposits, were not allowed to be taken out of the bank; the amount thus accumulated would be equal to the largest sum employed, at one period. This therefore made more bank money, at times, than was needed, and thereby it would cause it to depreciate.

This difficulty was met, very much in the same way that the Germans are said, in olden times, to have carried their grist to mill by tying a stone in one end of the bags to balance the grain in the other end—*i. e.* when they found the bank credits were being offered too freely in market, the bank brokers, purchased the surplus credits up at four per cent. premium, and sold them again at five; by this contrivance they managed to keep an even market, except on some extraordinary occasions.

Special deposits of coin were received, counted, weighed and put into a little sack—if gold it was sealed by the depositor.

The bank then gave him a receipt (recipisse) thus :

Amsterdam, 1. April, 1700.

John Burgher has deposited in Bank, one thousand Louis d'or upon condition that he may withdraw them within the space of six months, paying one-quarter per cent., or in default thereof, that they may be taken by the Bank at the rate above named.

No. 10,700   N. N.

For the Bank.

The depositor had the right to withdraw a special deposit, and that right could be extended indefinitely upon paying every six months a half of one per cent. for bullion; and a quarter per cent. on all coins, except ducatoons, for which were charged one-eighth. This specie deposit was credited in account to the depositor and by him transferable with its rights of withdrawal to others like other credits. Its value depended upon the kind of coin or bullion it represented.

Upon its withdrawal at any time within the six months specified, the recipisse was to be surrendered, and the bank credit transferred. The credits thus obtained might pass from hand to hand daily in payment of debts, while the recipisse was passing in like manner among the coin and bullion dealers or brokers.

The bank performed its functions satisfactorily, and the trouble of the coinage system was avoided.

In 1672, when the French army entered the low countries, and other places, the depositors alarmed for the safety of their deposits, although not entitled to withdraw them; yet upon a demand upon the bank, were permitted to do so. Those living at a distance, sold theirs at 5 and 6 per cent. discount; which with the premium they bore, made the loss 11 or 12 per cent. The French however, did not disturb the Bank, and its deposits were soon restored.

There were times when premiums on gold, or bullion deposits went up to 10 and even 12 per cent. Query, as it was all gold, was this premium on account of the currency inflation, or was it the gold inflation?

At such times the brokers drove a thriving business. Dealing in these *recipisses* required but little capital. A *recipisse* for instance of 1000 Louis d'or might sell for ten florins advance, and the Louis d'or be withdrawn by a transfer of the requisite bank credit. So in coin or bullion, deposited for payment of debts; the rise in value could thus by a special deposit be saved to the depositor. Fluctuations in the value of coin could thus be dealt in, without being obliged to hold the coin. The right to the coin, not the coin, was the subject matter of speculation. A competition was thus maintained without gold, speculation in gold, is not confined to this age. Stock gambling and gold gambling are the natural fruit of unjust and partial laws, if no such partial laws existed, no such excessive demands for gold would exist.

The Bank of Amsterdam, maintained its credit for about two centuries—its treasure has been estimated in amounts ranging from five to eighty millions pounds sterling. If it is put at ten millions, moved one hundred times a year, the payments thus made would amount to one billion pounds sterling, or $4,880,000,000, the transfers of this enormous sum was made continually year after year, during the long period of time the Bank flourished. But. in 1790, it was discovered that the larger portion of these deposits had been loaned out to the East In. Co., fifty years anterior to that time. Neither the provinces of Holland, nor the City of Amsterdam could make immediate restitution. This gross breach of trust caused the Bank to fail. But before this fraud was discovered transfers of these credits had been made by them for hundreds of millions pounds sterling per annum. Yet the efficiency and validity of the payments remained unquestioned. No change, no evil, no derangement of commerce occurred, in consequence of the fraud in the transaction of business, made during the fifty years next preceding the discovery, that the coin had been squandered.

By the transactions of this Bank then, as well as those of Venice and Genoa, it is shown that any desired amount of business can be satisfactorily done with the credit of property through the legalized agency of paper, under gavernmental management and control.

It is idle, therefore, to claim that a good paper cannot be furnished by the government, and it is equally absurd to claim that the exercise of the legitimate power by the government, will be more likely to lead to corruption than to loan out the government to the use of fifteen hundred soulless corporations for the purpose of enabling them to plunder the community for their own private gain.

CHAPTER VIII.

THE BANK OF HAMBURG.

The Bank of Hamburg is another institution of the same class with those of Amsterdam, Genoa and Venice, more nearly agreeing in its mode of institution and operation with the Bank of Amsterdam. It was founded in 1619, ten years after the Bank of Amsterdam. The same reasons existed for the formation of this Bank, that caused the formation of the three other Banks above named, viz.: a debased and diverse coinage. And what is singular in this case is, the fact, that while the Statesmen of the United States are seeking to establish a gold base, and a pretended specie paying system to rectify the adverse exchange; an adverse exchange on account of the diverse and debased coinage—the very reason assigned for the institution of the Bank of Hamburg, was the desire to get rid of this enormous evil.

One of the causes, and a leading cause for an unfavorable exchange was the circulation of this debased and diverse coin, which naturally flowed to the City of Hamburg, it being a free port. And this evil was so great, as to prove a serious damage to trade and commerce. The commercial men of Hamburg, therefore, very naturally followed the lead of Amsterdam, in shutting, or locking up the coin, as the only tangible mode of getting rid of such on intolerable evil as they had found this to be.

This Hamburg Bank at first adopted a rule to secure on deposit only the rix-dollars of the German Empire—a standard coin of silver. The officers vainly supposed by adopting this course, that the bank and the business community would escape the frauds and the evils caused by the whole army of counterfeiters, sweaters, pluggers and clippers, which are as much the product of this coinage system, as are the brokers, and gold gamblers, and all these classes, should be looked upon as the natural enemies of mankind, but which cannot be got rid of until the people shall demand and obtain just and equal laws.

But notwithstanding the Hamburghers imagined that by locking up the coin they should escape the meshes of these various fraudulent classes, as well as avoid the depredations of burglars, robbers and pirates. They soon found, however, that they had made a sad mistake—that the enemy they had feared and hoped to escape was still pursuing them, though it changed its 'form, it had not changed its fraudulent character, but was still in their midst, in the garb of a new national coin. The mint of the Empire it appears had caused to be largely issued a new coin of the same name and apparent value, but of a lower value than those first deposited in the Bank. Merchants who were in the secret managed to deposit the new coin, and withdraw the old. The new coin was worth about five per cent. less than the old. This disturbance caused the managers to close the bank for a time. An average of the loss by the discount on the new coin, was struck at about two and a half per cent., and the loss of all depositors was adjusted at that rate. There was no coin which this marc banco represented; but from 1770, it has continued to be the denominational unit of a money of account of the Bank.

The discovery of this fraud caused the managers to have every deposit duly assayed, or tested, and they gave credit on the bank books accordingly. The alloy in the standard adopted was as one to 47, fine gold. This Bank money has proved to be one of the most reliable, and subject to the least change of any in Europe.

It has for a long time bore a premium over coin, from twenty to twenty-five per cent. This demonstrates very clearly, that coin, though it may be used for the retail trade among civilized nations, does not answer the purpose for the large transactions of commerce. It is indeed very questionable, whether for the purposes of retail business, paper cannot be used at better advantage, and at less expense. The experiment which is now being tried in the United States, arising out of war, will it is believed settle this question decidedly in favor of paper as the best medium; even in small transactions of deal among the people.

And, so far as the foreign trade is concerned, all coin goes into the market simply as bullion—a mere commodity, governed by the same principles, as other commodities.

The officers of the Hamburg bank consisted of five directors, two counsellors, two treasurers, and two of the principal magistrates of the city. These constituted its official board, or government. The term of office, of one officer in each class, expires annually.

The vaults of the Bank have each five locks, and each director holds one key; so that it takes the whole five directors to open the bank treasury. No employee, and no broker, is permitted to open an account with the Bank. The Bank is for merchants and citizens. It has a loan office connected with it, where a loan may be made on a pledge of gold, silver and jewels, at three-fourths their value. The mint and coinage of the city is under the control of the Bank.

The credit of the Bank has remained almost uniformly good, though it was somewhat injured by the debased coin above mentioned. Davoust, one of Napoleon's marshalls, once took out all its money to pay his soldiers; but the French Government made restitution, and that restored the Bank. And it once loaned too much on pledges. These are all of the more serious difficulties, affecting its credit, which have occurred in the management of the Bank since its institution.

The rule which it has adopted, permitting only one transfer of the same sum daily, is the same as that adopted at Amsterdam. Transfers, or payments, are made from 7 to 10 o'clock A. M., and by paying for the privilege, from 10 to 1 P. M., and from 3 to 5 P. M. Enquiries as to whether transfers have been made, are governed by the same rule. These charges for giving information are generally compounded with the clerks and the information furnished during banking hours, at any period desired.

This bank still exists in full vigor, though its mode of business is somewhat cramped by its rules, limiting transfers of the sum to one day, yet it has proved a very efficient agent in making payments, and in avoiding many of the great evils resulting from coinage.

The use made of credits through the agency of the banks of Venice, Genoa, Amsterdam and Hamburg, are tangible evidence that the use of specie in making an exchange long since ceased— that the only essential use of the *precious metals*, is that of a commodity in settling balances. Being commodities they should be left like other commodities, to be accumulated or not accumulated, as shall suit the interest of those, who have occasion to deal in them.

No doubt, but that in settling balances, there is a great convenience in having so great and so uniform a value in so small a compass as is contained in these metals. But so long as foreign nations shall pursue the policy of holding up their value by coinage or mint regulations, we shall get the full benefit of those regulations.

This, therefore, furnishes the very best reason why the practical lessons taught by the history of the banks here named should be heeded. The paper money which under these systems has been so effective in making payments, should be rendered still more so. By being divorced from registering merely the fluctuations of gold, it can be made an accurate register of the price, and change of price of all commodities. Paper made a legal tender for all commodities, and not any one commodity, would dissolve this unnatural and monstrous union, between paper and gold. Neither the price of gold, or silver, can be controlled by legislation for any purpose but an evil one. The law of supply and demand, not legal requirements govern the market. But the excessive demand for these metals, which individuals or governments create by overtrading, or by partial laws, should be provided for by those who do the overtrading, and the wicked laws should not exist. Certainly, these evils should not through the medium of the currency be saddled upon those who want the money only to make an exchange of articles of their own production, and not those they do not have—then those who do the excessive dealing, or who buy the foreign goods, will make their own provision for these excesses, and nobody else will will suffer for their wrong.

CHAPTER IX.

BANK OF ENGLAND—ENGLISH BANKING.

Banking was introduced into England by the Lombard Jews, who brought the system with them from Italy. Banks were first established in Italy, in A. D. 808. These Jews who came from Lombardy, settled in London in a street which from that circumstance is called . Lombard street, where many bankers still reside. The name is derived from banco, a bench, which was erected in the market place for the exchange of money. "The mint in the Tower of London was anciently the depository for merchants' cash, until Charles I. laid his hands upon the money, and destroyed the credit of the mint in 1640. The traders were thereby driven to some other place of security for their gold, which, when kept at home, their apprentices frequently absconded with to the army. In 1645 therefore, they consented to lodge it with the goldsmiths in Lombard street, who were provided with strong chests for their own valuable wares; and this became the origin of banking in England."—Haydn. In 1694, the English Government was, and had been for a longtime, previously, badly embarrassed in its financial affairs, and by the efforts of William Patterson, an enterprising and scheming Scotchman, a charter for the Bank of England was obtained—it bears date 27th July, 1694. As this Bank is one of the leading institutions in the world, and is more frequently pointed to in this country as the great exemplar which it is necessary to follow, in order to establish a permanent system. It is important in any examination of the subject of paper money, that the essential principles upon which this institution rests should be thoroughly discussed. We are about to institute an entirely new system, under national authority. So far as legislation has as yet advanced, it is in line with the English system. It cannot therefore, be a matter of trivial importance to understand what that system is.

The Bank of England transacts the whole business of Government. "She acts not only," says Adam Smith, "as an ordinary bank, but as a great engine of state. She receives and pays the greater part of the annuities which are due to the creditors of the public; she circulates exchequer bills; and she advances to the government the annual amount of the land and malt taxes, which are frequently not paid till some years thereafter."

The Bank then being "an engine of state"—the first question which naturally arises, is its constitution and powers. The Charter among other things declares that "they shall be capable in law, to purchase, enjoy, and retain to them and their successors, any monies, lands, rents, tenements, and possessions whatsoever; and to purchase and acquire all sorts of goods and chattels whatever, wherein they are not restrained by the Act of Parliament; and also to grant, demise, and dispose of the same."

That the officers shall be, a governor and twenty-four directors, to be elected between the 25th of March, and the 25th day of April, in each year, from members duly qualified.

Stockholders must be natural born subjects of England, or naturalized subjects; must own in their own name for their own use severally, viz.: the governor at least £4,000, the deputy governor £3,000, and each director £2,000.

Every elector must have, in his own name, and for his own use, £500, or more, capital stock, and can only give one vote.

That thirteen or more of the said governors and directors, (of which the governor, or deputy-governor must always be one,) shall constitute a court of directors for the management of the affairs of the company, and for the appointment of all agents and servants, which may be necessary; paying them such salaries as they may consider reasonable.

Four general courts are to be held every year in the months of September, December, April and July. A general court may be summoned at any time, upon the requisition of nine proprietors duly qualified as electors.

"The corporation is prohibited from engaging in any sort of commercial undertaking, other, than dealing in bills of exchange, and in gold and silver. It is authorized to advance money upon the security of goods, wares, and merchandize, pledged to it; and to sell by public auction such goods as are not redeemed within a specified time."

By statute 6 Wiliam and Mary, it is also enacted, that the bank shall not deal in any goods, wares, merchandize (except bullion), or purchase any lands or revenues belonging to the crown, or advance or lend to their majesties, their heirs or successors any sums of money by way of loan or anticipation, or any part or parts, branch or branches, fund or funds of the revenue, now granted or belonging, or hereafter to be granted to their majesties, their heirs and successors, other than such fund or funds, part or parts, branch or branches of the said revenue only, on which a credit of loan is, or shall be granted by Parliament. And in 1697, it was enacted, that the common capital, or principal stock, and also the real fund of the governor and company, or any profit or produce to be made thereof, or arising thereby, *shall be exempted from any rates, taxes, assessments, or impositions whatsoever during the continuance of the bank ;* that all the profit, benefit, and advantage from time to time arising out of the management of the said corporation, shall be applied to the use of all the members of the said association of the governor and company of the Bank of England, rateably and in proportion to each member's part, share, and interest in the common capital and principal stock of the said governor and company hereby established."

The foregoing presents the leading provisions or grants of power with all its limitations. While these powers are very broad, the Bank is nowhere directly authorized to issue bank bills—and a writer who has given a history of its origin, says : "That the Bank of England crept into the world, not being in any votes (proposed laws) by that name, but an act ; granting to their Majesties several duties upon tonnage of ships, beer, ale, etc., for securing certain recompenses to such as should subscribe £1,200,000 on a fund of eight per cent.

Patterson knowing that the government being then engaged in war, was in great straits, and was frequently obliged to pay from ten to forty per cent. interest for money, made it a permanent portion of his scheme to offer the government a loan of £1,200,000, at eight per cent. interest.

It was this, that secured a hearing for this project. It is probable that while Patterson was the active man engaged in pushing forward the scheme, that there were others less prominent who were no less active and effective in carrying this measure through Parliament. It appears that Michael Godfrey, one of the active promoters of the enterprise had obtained

£500,000 subscription to the stock before the passage of the Act. The remaining £700,000 was, upon due notice given, under the charter subscribed in ten days after opening the books.

The bank went into operation, January 1st, 1695. Its whole capital was lent to the government as a special loan—the interest was secured by certain specified taxes mentioned in the charter· The sum of £4,000, was added to the £96,000 interest paid the bank, as a compensation for managing the loan.

Thus the power of England culminated in its Bank, and the annual industry of the people was pledged to support it. Although the bank charter was passed by Parliament under a false title— containing as it did an enormous grant of power, and an entire exemption from taxation, yet it did not get into operation without these wrongs being discovered and thoroughly denounced.

The writer quoted, among other things asserts: " That if it had been known what kind of a bank was wrapped up in that bill, many persons would have been willing to lent the government the money for several years gratis to have obtained such a charter."

Another writer says : "The nation had been for several years engaged in an expensive, hazardous and doubtful war; the government had drained all their projects to raise the necessary supplies; but the credit of the nation sunk, occasioned partly by the divisions of Parliament, the deficiency of the funds, and most unfortunately by the baseness of our coin, so that neither our money, nor our credit would pass in market....And when such an enemy was at our doors, it was too favorable an opportunity for such a fort as this to be erected, which, though then designed for our defence, serves now, (1707) to overawe us, and has turned its cannon against the state it was built to protect.... We are, God be thanked, greatly recovered from that dangerous crisis, our credit retrieved, our money recoined, great part of our debts paid, and almost all provided for."....We crowd more to get our money into the funds, than heretofore to get it out; and we are freed from any necessity of supporting the wants of the government. It is therefore, a matter of prudence, whether the bank ought to be continued longer." ...He concludes as follows: "If they, (the people) would have their power and liberties safe, by putting it out the power of any to molest them, and by keeping their elections free, not to repair this fort (The Bank of England), that overawes them, and by their compassion to the poor tradesmen, and their own interest, not to establish iniquity by law."

This writer seems to labor under the impression that the question of right could have something to do with the establishing, or not establishing the Bank. When the Act shows that the Bank was established as an engine of power to accomplish for those in power the very object against which this writer declaims, viz. : to hold the power of the government absolutely in the hands of those who control the Bank. This it has so effectually done, that neither reason, justice, nor anything short of revolution, can remove or change this Bank power. To change or remove this power is to change the Government itself, and the false, arbitrary, and unjust principle upon which it is based. And this principle is, that government is mainly instituted for the benefit of the governing class. This object is clearly to be seen in the mode of instituting the Bank, in the powers granted, and in its practical operations as delineated by its whole history.

It has already been shown, that the Act of Incorporation did not confer a special power to issue bank-notes, or other paper, to circulate as money. By a notice dated February 11th, 1695, notice was given, that the three cashiers named were the only persons authorized to give notes on behalf of the company, either for payment of money or bills ; for which the bank was, or would be accountable.

The first issues of paper were for £20. In 1696, during the difficulties arising out of a national recoinage, the Bank suspended specie payments, and resorted to issuing bills under seal, payable on demand, bearing six per cent. interest with these bills it redeemed the notes previously issued by the bank, known as cashiers' notes payable on demand, without interest.

These sealed bills, cashier's notes, and cash, on the 10th of November, 1696, were as follows : Sealed bills, £893,800; cashier's notes, £764,196 ; cash on hand, £35,664. This was a sorry sum with which to meet in payment £1,657,996 of sealed bills and notes. That the loans had been made principally to the government, is evidenced by the fact, that only £231,000 had been loaned to individuals. To remove the insolvency of the Bank, the Government allowed it to take up its liabilities by a fresh issue of capital stock. The credit of the government at this time, stood at a discount of from forty to fifty per cent., and bank-notes from twelve to twenty per cent.

The new issue of stock amounted to £1,000,171, which with the original capital made a subscribed capital of £2,201,171.

This large increase of capital would have naturally added to the credit of the Bank. But the depreciated condition of the public stocks, and the bills of the Bank furnished an opportunity to strengthen the power of the Bank, and to rob the people, too valuable not to be improved. Accordingly Parliament passed the following strengthening Act, before alluded to, viz.: that "the common capital and principal stock, and also the real fund of the government and company, or any profit or produce to be made thereof, or arising thereby, shall be exempted from any rates, taxes, assessments, or impositions whatsoever; during the continuance of the Bank, etc.

This with the increase of capital raised the stock in a few months to 112 per cent., enhanced the value of the government securities, gave the bank notes free currency, and thus, by this aid, the Bank soon recovered from the effects of its suspension.

In 1708, the directors undertook to pay off and cancel £1,500,000 exchequer bills, issued two years before, which with interest amounted to £1,775,038, this increased the debt, which the government owed the Bank to £3,275,028 at six per cent. interest. The government then allowed the Bank to double its capital which increased the amount to £4,402,343, and this was the occasion for another supplemental Act to strengthen the Bank, this provides that "it shall not be lawful for any body politic, erected, or to be erected, other than the said governor and company of the Bank of England, or of any other persons whatsoever, united or to be united in covenants or partnership, exceeding the number of six persons, in that part of Great Britain called England, to borrow, owe, or take up any sum or sums of money on their bills, or notes payable on demand, or in any less time than six months, from the borrowing thereof."

This proviso virtually placed the whole circulation of demand notes in the hands of the Bank, and as might have been anticipated, it had a powerful operation on banking, in England. It is claimed that this Act was elicited by the Mine-Adventure Company having commenced banking business, and begun to issue notes. But that may have been the occasion, or a pretence for passing the Act. Yet the design of creating the Bank of England from the beginning was to make it an engine of power; and step by step that design has been carried out.

As the Bank had nothing in its vaults, but certificates of the public debt to the amount of £1,200,000, it had but three modes of business left open to be pursued:

1. To lend the money of its depositors, or
2. To issue its own notes, or
3. To employ its credit in discounting bills of exchange and promissory notes, by a credit to its customers upon the books of the bank, for the proceeds of paper discounted, and allowing the parties to transfer them to others, in such sums as their business might demand.

The credit of the Bank after the increase of its stock, and the exemption of its capital from taxation, stood very high, notwithstanding the disturbance caused by its suspension the second year after its institution.

All the above named modes of business were combined together in the operations of the bank, though each are essentially distinct, and must be so considered, in order to get clear ideas upon the subject.

A provision for the safe-keeping, holding, and paying out money is very ancient. When this money is coin, the masses of men have not sufficient practice in dealing, weighing and testing of coins, or of bullion, to enable them safely to deal in them. Hence in every commercial community there is a class of men who become skilled in handling and testing the qualities of these metals, and these persons in the early ages were naturally the goldsmiths whose business and wares made them adepts in testing qualities, and repositors of coin and bullion. The Saviour, in the parable, makes the lord of the unfaithful servant say: "Wherefore then gavest not thou thy money into the bank, that at my coming, I might have required mine own, with usury." This clearly indicates that the practice of depositing money with the bankers, and paying interest upon it, was prevalent at that time.

The goldsmiths of England, at the time the Bank was chartered, had been, and were a long time afterwards bankers, or depositories for others. But as Charles the First and Second, had committed extensive robberies upon these bankers; their ability safely to keep the money entrusted to them, was doubted.

The Bank of England, therefore, from its extensive franchises, and capital, was able at once to command public confidence sufficient to secure it large deposits. One by-law required the cash should be carefully kept under three or more locks; the keys

7

whereof shall be kept by such three or more Governors, Deputy-Governor, and Directors; as the said Court of Directors shall from time to time empower to keep the same, each of said persons keeping one of said keys."

This provision increased the confidence in the Bank as a place of security, and naturally attracted a large number of depositors to deposit, who only desired to use their deposits in such amounts as the ordinary demands of business required. This would leave a large amount of money in the Bank, which the owners would not be likely soon to want.

These deposits under the theory of banking, belong to the banker; subject to payment on demand in like money. In Europe, and in this country, from the earliest periods of their history, the practice of loaning these deposits has been universal. The great gains in banking are largely from this source. As the aggregation of money is largely for the purposes of gain through interest, and the control it gives over the value of products. When these are plenty, and business prosperous, bankers conclude that as money comes in rapidly, their *interest* requires that it should go out with equal rapidity, to keep up an equilibrium. But the accelerated motion soon reaches its end—a crash, and depositors find to their sorrow that while banks are convenient depositories for money in sunshine; they are not to be relied upon for a return of deposits in a storm.

The Bank of England, like other banks, on securities, loans its deposits, and like other banks, as will be shown, at times is not able upon demand to return them to the owners. Many such instances have occurred in its history. But as the Bank through taxes and interest, is enthroned on the annual industry of the nation, it sooner recuperates than private banks. Through governmental aid it has been enabled to sustain itself in its financial disasters; apparently, without loss to the individual. The injury is thereby saddled upon the nation; and not upon the individual. His deposits are safe, though business is ruined.

For a hundred and seventy-five years however no depositor in the Bank of England, has ever lost his deposit. While during that period, by the failure of private bankers; immense sums have been totally lost. This safety of deposits, has given the Bank a very great advantage over private bankers. The Bank has made immense sums, out of this branch of its business, in loaning deposits; and this branch of business has been constantly increasing in magnitude and advantage; up to this time.

This presents only the simple question, of the advantage which the Bank derived, from being deemed a more safe depository of coin and bullion, than any private bank could be, and the superior facilities thereby furnished, for loaning deposits, and not to endanger the rights of depositors.

It has been deemed advisable to separate the functions and processes of the bank; not only for the purpose. of giving a better understanding of the subject of banking, as a whole, but because banking as it now exists in the United States, takes its form from the Bank of England. In this Bank too, is concentrated, not only all that is claimed to be useful in the systems which preceded it; but it certainly contains all, that is overreaching and destructive, to the rights of the people.

It was also; not only the culminating point of the despotism of the past; but it was the ushering in of a system, which while it released the bankers and financiers from many of the responsibilities and guarrantees of former systems; it enabled them to obtain a double rent, or interest, for furnishing mere counters, or tallies, of the people's property; and by which, it could be exchanged.

Henceforth cheating in coinage, robbing bankers and depositors by the Henry's, and the Charles's, was also at an end. Even counterfeiting, robbing, cheating, plugging, sweating and boring, outside of bank franchises, had become contemptibly mean and insignificant. The Bankers and financiers were now to divide the spoils with the King and Parliament; and even a limit was put upon the Kings right to obtain more than his allotted share of the spoils, without consent of Parliament. And the legitimate use of coin is now, to be locked up in capacious vaults, to settle balances of trade, and to cover up, and hide the unmitigated and unparalleled robbery of the new system. This feat could only be accomplished, by making the people believe, that the gold which the bankers do not use, and generally do not possess, is the real and only base of their system, when in fact the system was established in its present form to avoid the use of gold.

It is therefore important, not only that the boundary lines between the old and the new financial system, should be distinctly marked, and pointed out, but it is also necessary, in a work which professedly treats on money, that the outlines or distinct processes of both systems should be accurately marked and well defined.

It should be borne in mind, that up to this period of time, no regular system of bank bills for any certain defined amount, had ever been instituted. The title to coin, instead of coin, and the debt of the State, had been long, and extensively used, as money by the banks of Venice and Genoa, and with much more efficiency, than coin and bullion. The latter bank had also issued bank bills extensively as money; but not in any defined and regular denominations as is now being done.

In England too, bills of exchange and promissory notes—payable at some future specified time, had been extensively used as a circulating medium, but nothing in the form of bank-bills had ever been issued. And it has been shown, that while the Bank Charter was perhaps one of the most grasping, overreaching grants of power ever enacted. Yet, it nowhere expressly grants the power, to issue bank-notes.

When therefore the Bank-Government, had obtained a heavy amount of indebtedness of the State; as a security for their advances, as well as a base for their future bank operations, with a large proportion of the annual productions of the people thereby secured, as a revenue, and with a corresponding large increase of their capital stock, they were then prepared to take another step forward, in line with the Genoese Bank. And that advance step was, to issue bank-bills payable on demand, in regular denominations of value, and in amount sufficient to furnish a full supply, for the major part of the circulation of money, in all the transactions of business in the commercial world.·

To the uninitiated this was undoubtedly a bold stroke of policy, not easily understood. We may well suppose, that the old gold or bullion-theorists, savans, statesmen and financiers, outside the Bank-government-ring, must have been startled as with an electric shock; at the mere announcement of such an extraordinary doctrine—the gods of the banker, and the gods of the people, were by this bank-paper issue to be consigned to the tomb of the Capulets, or to a bank vault oblivion.

But that the issue of paper, as money, was designed by the originators of the Bank from the beginning, is evident from the nature and character of the powers granted by the Charter, and by the Acts of the Bank-Government-Court; immediately succeeding the organization of the Bank   The Bank-govern-

ment, well understood the history of the Bank of Genoa, its issue
of paper as money, and had in many particulars copied after that
institution.

On the 16th of January, 1695, the Bank was organized, and
on the 11th of February the same year it issued a notice, that the
three cashiers named were the only persons authorized to give
notes for the payment of money or bills; and on the 10th of
November 1696, it appears by a statement furnished to the
House of Commons, that there was then outstanding cashier's
notes, payable on demand, not bearing interest £764,196, sealed
bills £873,800, and on the 28th February, 1698, there was outstanding and unpaid notes and post bills, amounting to
£1,221,290. And in 1708 the Bank obtained an Act restricting
the issuing of bills or notes payable on demand by any persons
exceeding six in number, except the Bank of England, and as
above stated.

From all these facts combined then it is fair to infer that however ignorant the public may have been as to the Bank's intention
to issue paper money, the stockholders of the Bank understood
and intended it from the commencement.

Bank-notes as now issued, were unknown among business men
in England, when the Bank was instituted. Goldsmiths and
commercial men had issued promissory notes, payable on
demand; but these were never regarded as money or currency.
And the Bank-notes in common parlance, in business and in
public documents continued for a long time to be called promissory notes, payable on demand, to distinguish between these and
those drawn payable at some future time.

The view which was taken of these demand-notes now called
bank-bills, by the Bank-Board, may present the subject in the
light in which it ought to be presented. The Charter authorized
the Bank to deal in bills of exchange, domestic and foreign.
These were much used, and of course soon found their way into
the Bank. The amount of these bills far exceeded all the coin
and bullion in the country, and the amount thus offered to the
Bank opened up a bnsiness far exceeding any operations which
could be effected through the use of coin or bullion. The
question thereby presented was, how could the bank deal in
these bills, benefit themselves, and accommodate the commercial
public.

Bills of exchange and promissory notes were then, as now,

payable at some future day, generally from three to six months after date. These instruments by way of payment, were of no use to the holders until maturity; unless they could be used as collaterals in procuring a loan of money. But as the Bank had a use for all the money it had, these could not be rendered available for present use through that channel.

If, however, the bank could take a prommissory note, or bill of exchange, due at ninety days for £500, and cut it up into twenty-five £20 notes, which could be presently used in making payments that would be a decided advantage to the business public, as more or less of notes and bills of this character were held among business men. Although this paper was not due, and therefore upon an advance made upon it, no dependence could be placed on the paper for re-imbursement, until its maturity. Yet the Bank-Governors, under the pressure of the love of gain, and by the advice of financiers, interested in the bank, concluded to discount this paper, and to give in its place, their own notes payable on demand. And, without the coin, to be able to meet their promise to pay thus to abolish the intervening time, which· the note or bill had to run, before payment could be demanded.

It was alleged in favor of this mode of business, that it would greatly add to, and facilitate commercial business, and that these notes, would pass into circulation throughout the nation so extensively; and would be so necessary for the transactions of the domestic trade, that they would not, and could not be returned to the bank suddenly, in sufficiently large quantities, to embarrass the Bank.

Reasoning of this character, so far influenced or controlled the action of the Bank-Court, that it determined to issue notes of the Bank, payable on demand, in exchange for individual notes, and bills, payable at a future day. These notes being payable to bearer on demand, did not require an endorsement to pass them from one person to another.

Under the theory upon which money, and banking was then, and is now instituted; the Bank could not have more effectually destroyed the very principle upon which· it was pretended to be based. It undertook and promised to pay on demand millions of pounds sterling. when there was not a single pound which could lawfully be appropriated to make that payment. This was not simply a moral fault, but under the theory of banking it was a grave crime. Because, if paper money is only good, by virtue of the gold to redeem the paper with, then to issue it, knowing that the Bank did not have the money with which to redeem it, was certainly a most gross fraud. The Bank undertook to perform, what it knew was an impossibility to be performed, under the delusive idea, that the *money* (paper) issued would not have to be redeemed. It could have issued its own paper in smaller denominations, and made it payable at the same time that the individual paper it received, was made payable, without any serious risk; and by its superior credit would have thereby rendered the public a great service in so doing. It certainly could not demand coin, on the paper received, until it was due, and by no kind of legerdemain yet discovered; could it pay coin or bullion by promising so to do; when it had no coin wherewith to pay. If the bank paper had been payable on the day the individual paper was payable, then the bank paper could have easily been made to pay the individual paper. The Bank could at least have received back its own paper in payment for the paper of individuals, and thus the whole transaction would have been settled and paid, without the use of either gold or silver. This is the way practically, in which all the bank paper of the world is at present circulated, redeemed, or paid.

If, for instance the Bank had received notes and bills to the amount of £10,000,00 having ninety days to run at a discount of six per cent., it could then have issued, its own notes, due at ninety days, in denominations of £20 each, for £9,850,000, the amount due the business public for the bank-bills: the discount having been deducted.

The holders of these bank-bills would hold them in place of the £10,000,000 of paper transferred to the bank for its bills; thus put into circulation. This would have furnished a good circulating medium backed by the whole power of the government. The debtors then for the £10,000,000, of notes, and bills of exchange, held by the Bank, would have had to obtain back again from the public the £9,850,000 bank-bills issued by the Bank, and £150,000 coin, or bullion, which had been discounted from the principal for interest. This amount, would have paid off their whole indebtedness to the Bank. The public in this way would have obtained a good, honest, circulating medium, of uniform value; based solely upon the government, and the property, which had been exchanged by it. Through the agency of the purchase, the notes and bills were full security and payment for the property purchased, and notes of the Bank; given for the notes and bills of individuals would be a good payment to the Bank, for these notes and bills thus held.

But in the case supposed, the Bank under its theory would have issued £9,850,000 bank-notes, due in coin or bullion on demand. When the only fund it had for the redemption of this sum of money, was the £10,000,000 due at ninety days after date. The demand notes of the Bank having no present fund for their redemption, would have been, and were a fraud, and a lie, upon their face. And every bank-note issued upon such a base, from the day that the Bank of England issued her first demand, or bank-note, down to the present time, is *a public lie* and a *public fraud*, sanctified and made honorable, only, by almost two hundred years legislation.

If, however, the bank paper was issued, as in the case first above supposed, then the debtor, with one and a half per cent. coin, or bullion added to the Banks own paper, and which had been previously issued for the debtor's paper, would have taken up that paper. Neither bank, nor debtors, had paid coin for it. Neither the debtor's paper, or the bank-paper, represented or denoted coin; but goods, wares, merchandize, products and labor. No coin had been used, or was needed in making these purchases, and it was not needed to give any validity, power, or value, to the bank-notes, or the notes and bills of exchange, which had been given in exchange for the property. The bills of exchange, and promissory notes, paid for the property purchased. The bank-bills were given by the Bank in exchange for these, and the bank-bills were a just payment to the Bank, for the same paper, for which they had been previously exchanged.

It is claimed, however, that some pretended connection of this bank-paper, with coin and bullion as a base, is necessary to check over-issue of bank-paper, in other words, that the property for which this paper is originally issued, and for the exchange of which property, it is solely issued, is not a good fund upon which to rely for redemption of the paper. If, however, as has been seen, the paper issued by the Bank, and circulated, is made as in the case supposed, it denotes simply the property it exchanges, then no such *base* pretence as a "gold base" is necessary, and that no such base has ever existed in fact, is fully attested by sad experience, of nearly two hundred years, both in Europe, and in this country.

There are modes of issuing paper money however, which are both honest and safe, and which therefore needs no counter-checks to prevent over-issues. Indeed, no over-issues would occur, under an honest system. One of these modes which has been thoroughly tested, is the circulation of a public debt. The efficiency of this mode of furnishing a currency, was fully demonstrated by the Bank of Venice. Its success has never yet been equalled. The only modification of that system, which an advancing civilization requires, is the substitution of treasury-certificates for a credit on the books of a bank, and the state, or government itself, should be substituted for the Bank. The debt itself, cut up into bills, called greenbacks, or legal money, would have furnished and would still furnish the most perfect, cheap, uniform, and just money ever instituted for the reason that it could be backed up by the property of the nation, sustained by just laws.

The Bank of England had this public debt in large amounts, and if British statesmen and the Bank-Court had desired a really good and reliable medium of exchange, instead of private gain, and the creation of an *engine of power*—that boon was then—and is now, within their reach. They could always have given the public debt, cut up into legal-tender notes, or treasury-certificates in such denominations as would suit the demands, or the convenience of the business public.

If the Bank had even, only been required to pay its notes in specie *pari passu* with the payment of the note, individual, or public liability for which the Bank paper had been issued—the Bank could have complied with that requisition.

If, however, specie is so essential (which is denied) to the validity and use of the bank-note, it can be secured by making it payable in gold or silver coin only, at two, three, or six months, when the time expires at which, the specie must be had to meet both demands—the specie paid on the securities could then be paid, if necessary, for the bank-note. And it was the only practical way, it could have been done.

It may be very convenient, to be able to demand specie when-ever it is wanted for any useful purpose, but it is a costly convenience to require it by law, when it is not needed or wanted for any purpose, but merely to satisfy the demands of an arbitrary law. Especially so, when law-makers know, or ought to know, that compliance with such a demand, upon the principle, upon which the Bank of England is instituted, and the manner in which business must be done, under such a law, is frequently, simply, an utter impossibility.

It would be a very great convenience frequently, for a hungry man who wants a dinner to-day, to be able to get such a daguerrotype likeness of his dinner, to be furnished at ninety days hence, that would satisfy the cravings of hunger of the present moment. But such a convenience under known laws could not reasonably be 'expected. Yet, it would be as reasonable an expectancy, as the issue of demand-notes for three-month-notes, and to expect these demand-notes, would not be presented for payment—or to expect the ninety-day-notes, or national-bonds, will furnish the specie to meet the requirements of to-day.

The principle which gives to paper-money whatever of efficiency it possesses, is the balancing power of credit, not coin. If A. buys of B. £10,000 worth of goods, or lands, and gives his notes for that sum, payable at ninety days, the best fund with which to pay A.'s £10,000, is B.'s *notes*, and if B. transfers these notes to the Bank for its paper, then the Bank-notes, are the best fund to pay B.'s notes to the Bank, and this is the principle which underlies this whole banking-system.

But ever since the institution of the Bank of England, and its paper-issue, it has always been claimed, that the safety of bank.paper, depends upon having a certain relative proportion preserved, between the amount of paper-money issued, and the coin or bullion, to be kept on hand for the purposes of redemption, and one-third seems to be the amount, which is generally relied on as a safe proportion.

Experiments based upon this principle. have continued to be made in England, from the institution of the Bank, and from that day, to this, and have cost the people ten times more, than all the advantages to be derived from the hoarded coins; and in the end have proved the whole system, to be a magnificent failure.

Undoubtedly the same principle should be applied to money, whether it is aggregated, or held by the individual, as is applied to every other commodity in every other branch of business.

If a penny-sheet of paper, will make as good an instrument of title, to transfer a farm worth $10,000, as would a piece of gold worth ten thousand dollars also, then paper should be used for that purpose; and if a farm can be transferred in that manner, so can the products of that farm, and every other commodity, and the gold is not essential for any such purpose. But it does not thence follow, that paper can supply the place of the farm, in production, nor that it can supply the place of gold as a commodity—but every function which gold performs as money, can be equally well performed by paper and at not a tithe of the expense, or cost of gold. Gold and silver, like other commodities, should be furnished and used for any purpose for which they are designed.

The wrong committed by the Bank of England, was: First; in agreeing to pay their notes in specie, when it did not have the specie with which to pay; second, in issuing notes, payable on demand, to be exchanged for notes having two, three, and four months to run, when the only fund for the redemption of the bank-notes, was these individual notes.

No excuse can justify such an act. Individuals cannot honestly transact business in this manner, neither can corporations, or banks.

If the Bank had issued only its notes, payable on demand, that it was prepared to redeem, or if on time, not payable sooner than the paper taken in exchange for its notes, then no suspension of specie payments would have occurred, nor would its business require its circulation to fluctuate with the demand for gold, for exportation to meet the foreign demand. Hence the internal trade would not continually be deranged if not destroyed, to enable the Bank to meet the requirements of the foreign commerce. All legitimate trade through whatever medium effected, is a mere exchange of articles. The natural wants of man must be supplied with, or without gold, or silver, as occasion may require. It is a great fallacy to imagine that the medium of exchange must fluctuate in supply, as the precious metals fluctuate in quantity. Both, in the domestic and foreign trade, commodities are principally distributed through the medium of promissory notes, and bills of exchange, very little use is made of either coin or bullion, except to settle balances, and these are comparatively small. The use of these metals even for this purpose, in civilized nations unless engaged in some special branch of trade, or whose industries have been disturbed by war, or some similar unnatural cause, are very limited indeed. But issuing bank-notes together with the whole business of banking, is a monstrous monopoly. Its profits in comparison with the service rendered are enormous. Concealment of the gross outrages inflicted by the system upon the rights of the people is absolutely necessary for the further continuance of the wrong. Hence its complicated legal machinery, and the ostentatious display of securities, and of gold and silver.

In England, and in this country, the gold and silver base idea, and the promise to redeem are kept constantly before the people. The very frauds of the system itself, are used to instil into their minds the importance of these false ideas.

For the purpose then of exposing this popular delusion, and bringing the people to see, that it is their deposits, and their property, or its avails, which furnishes the capital—that the enrichment of the banker, and capitalists, at their expense by law, is the object of the system.

We have shown, that deposits constituted the only available capital of the Bank of England. That its funds were loaned to the Government, and the issue of bank-notes, in the first instance not on gold and silver, but upon promissory notes and bills of exchange which had not even the poor merit of being due. It was for the purpose of speculating in these securities, that these bills were first issued in large quantities. Through this same instrumentality the practice is not only continued, but ninety-nine dollars out of every hundred of the fund for redemption of these bank-notes, comes from securities given for the people's property, and lodged in the Bank.

If it is not seen, that the potency of the bank-paper, is derived from the necessity of having it to meet the demand for the payment of the notes lodged with the Bank, when there is no other fund for their redemption. Certainly the suspension of the Bank for twenty-five years, will demonstrate the fact beyond the power of successful contradiction.

Whatever may have been the designs of the originators of the Bank at the outset—without doubt they intended to make use of the immense powers granted in their charter in every way in which such use could be rendered available as a matter of profit. And both they and their customers soon perceived that the use of *credits in account*, were much more effective in making payments, than by the circulation both of bank-notes and coin.

The discount of business paper, and the credit in account

soon far exceeded bank-notes and coin deposits. The bank, by this simple method, became the bookkeeper of its customers ; at least to the several amounts discounted for them.

It charged the same discount for a credit in account that it did upon a loan of coin, or bank-notes. This soon became the most important, as well as the most profitable, branch of its business. Keeping accounts was not so expensive as issuing notes. No distinction was made, however, in the account as to the source from whence the credit originated, nor was there any distinction made between that and coin or bank bills as to the use to be made of the credit in payment of debts. These credits, therefore, answered the same purpose in making payments as coin or bank-notes.

£20,000 in private notes, could not be made available in payment of debts—deposited in Bank £19,800, could be as effective in making purchases or payments, as would be so much coin.

This business was of course profitable to the Bank, but it involved a heavy risk. For by being thus credited, it became immediately payable in coin, which the Bank did not have.

As has been shown, if this credit had been payable only at the maturity of the paper for which the credit had been given—this was as far as the Bank could safely go, and this would have answered every legitimate purpose of credit, and that was all that the Bank had to grant. A more convenient mode of adjusting the large demands of commerce, could not well be devised. It combined all the advantages of set-off, rapid circulation and safety. It required no meeting of debtor and creditor to adjust accounts, no risk of bank-notes, counterfeiting, theft, robbery, or fire.

The merchant with his order or check could at any time make all his payments, if he desired, without the trouble of leaving his counting-room.

The Bank by this credit on their books, had after the example of the Banks of Venice and Genoa, inaugurated a system, by which without either gold or silver bullion, or even bank-bills, the payments in large, as well as in the smaller transactions of commerce could be made.

The Bank of England, therefore, it will be readily seen, is the fruitful parent of all the modern heresies, and robberies included in banking. "A gold base," "elasticity," and "convertibility of a currency," and other similar cabalistic terms used to cover up the wholesale swindling and out-right robbery of modern banking, are from the same source.

These periodical revulsions and financial disasters, which occur every few years have the same common parentage. The Bank of England first established these false theories respecting money. It first issued notes, payable on demand, and gave credits, or exchanged them for securities payable at a future day, varying in time from one to four months, yet relying wholly upon the forbearance of the public, not to present them for payment in sufficient quantities, to embarrass the operations of business.

Banks from that period of time down to the present, have continued to issue notes payable on demand, to be exchanged for time-securities, payable at from one, to four months after date, just as was, and is now being done by the Bank of England. These bills or notes, while they bear no interest, bring interest to the Bank. Interest though it produces nothing, accumulates much faster than the increase of property by the annual productions of labor. Besides, there is no provision made, for an increased issue of notes, to answer the increased demand, to pay the constantly cumulating interest.

If then the issue of paper to-day, is sufficient to answer all the legitimate demands of business; twelve months hence, from increased production, and for the reason here mentioned, it may fall far short of supplying the demands of business; and to return to the lender his principal and interest. Each returning year is liable to answer, not only its demands for money, but the cumulative interest of preceding years, until at last, a failure of crops, or adverse foreign exchange, brings the business community, as well as the banks satisfactory evidence, not only that bank money upon such a base, needs redemption, but that every man who deposits his money in bank, needs his own, to a much greater extent than is in the power of the bank to supply. The result is, that the business of the country soon gives way beneath these accumulated burthens. A collapse, or a financial crash follows. Manufacturing ceases, trade languishes, business comes to a dead stand, disappointment, poverty, wretchedness and ruin, follow in their train. The business community are gravely told, that there has been too much speculation, too much manu-facturing, too many engaged in the same business, too much production. In short, too much of everything, but an honest, reliable money, instituted at cost, and solely for the purpose of making a just exchange of this there is not too much. But what is the difficulty with the banker's *money?* The currency is inflated. There is too much paper afloat, and not gold enough to redeem it, say the bankers. But how stood the gold account for the long years previous to this when the paper was issued? Was there then gold sufficient to redeem the paper? We answer nay. There was gold on deposit to be sold as a commodity for use, or to settle balances of trade, but as has been shown not a dollar for redemption of the paper, and very seldom is there a dollar really issued on gold, except it is deposited as is required by the Bank of England. This Bank issues £14,000,000, based entirely on national bonds, if it issues above that amount it is upon a deposit of gold. But it has also been seen, that the amount of payments made by a simple credit on the books of the Bank, far exceeds both the issue of bank-paper, and the deposits of coin and bullion.

Where then, we again enquire, is the gold-base? The paper on the £14,000,000 bonds, is not pretended to be based on gold, neither is the credit on the books of the Bank, by which a much larger amount of payments are made. Where then is the inflation? There is no more inflation when the demand for redemption is made, than there was when the money was issued. The only difference is, that gold, which the Bank never had, is demanded, and was not required when the Bank made the issue. Does any one enquire that if this is true, how could this paper have been so long, and so extensively circulated? We answer, because the great operations of commerce are not carried on by gold and silver, but by CREDIT. It was so carried on in the 17th century, as we have already shown, in the case of the Banks of Venice and Genoa, it is so carried on to-day.

Merchandize and raw materials were at the origin of the Bank of England, as now, purchased and sold for promissory notes and bills of exchange. Changing these securities into bank-notes, complicated, but did not change the character of the transaction. There has been no time since the dawn of civilization, when there were not in the hands of individuals, notes and bills of exchange to represent the chief transactions of commerce. The average time of this credit may have been from two to four months. Whatever it may have been, there were always bills of exchange and promissory notes extant to show that individuals had undertaken to pay every specific sum in a certain specified time. To some extent this paper was always circulated in making purchases and payments, but its use was always limited either to intimate acquaintances, or to the guarranty of the seller, or obligee, named in the paper.

It was upon paper of this class, which could not have been less than £5,000,000, that the Bank of England commenced its paper-issues. On the continent various expedients had been resorted to for the purpose of making this paper available in purchases and payments without the use of coin. The Banks of Venice and Genoa, had to a great extent utilized this paper for these purposes. And the large exchanges of commerce in Europe and Asia too, had at, and previous to this period of time been effected through the instrumentality of public fairs. The same mode is still pursued to some extent, though much less than formerly. Yet they occupy a somewhat prominent place on the confines of Europe and in Asia.

The Russians sell or exchange with the Chinese, in fairs held at Kiachta, in Mongolia, their furs, skins, Russia leather, woolen cloths, German and Russian heavy linens, cattle and precious metals, for silk, raw, and manufactured, porcelains, sugar, rhubarb, nankins, etc.

Merchants found it a convenient mode, of making payments at these fairs. Bills of exchange were accordingly made payable at the various fairs, which were held at intervals of from three to twelve months. The fairs accordingly regulated the time, and furnished the means of payment.

The modes of payment differed according to the custom of the place where the fair was held. Those made at the city of Lyons, in France, will serve as a model for the rest. There were four fairs held here every year. Kings or Epiphany began in January, Easter in April; August in that month; and All Saints in November; Four "PAYMENTS" were also held, one for each fair. The Epiphany payments were held, all March; those of Easter, all June; those of August, all September; and those of Easter, all November. Engagements to a vast amount, arising out of other transactions besides those occurring at the fairs were made payable at these Payments, by bills of exchange, book accounts, and otherwise.

An account was here opened for all in their books with each Payment by name. This exhibited what sum each accountant had to pay, and what was due to each. The balance of this account determined what each person had to pay more than he was to receive, or to receive more than he was to pay. Bills payable at future Payments were thus expressed: "Pay to A. B. at next Easter Payment, etc." If Easter fair had then commenced, if to be paid at that fair, "at the current Easter Payments." Those who could not attend sent a duly authorized agent. "Every Payment was opened with ceremony. The *Provost Marchand* came to the exchange with his Register and six Syndics—two French—two Italians—and two Swiss, or Germans, and these after a short discourse to the assistants, recommending probity in trade, and observance of the laws, customs, and usages of the place, and these were then read, and the clerk drew up a *process verbal* of the opening of the Payment. Savary thus describes it:

"It is admirable to see the manner in which bankers and merchants of Lyons make their acceptances and payments among themselves of the bills of exchange which they draw, and which are remitted to them from every part of Europe, payable at the Payments, for there will be paid sometimes in two or three hours a million of livres, without disbursing a penny in money—that is indeed surprising to those who do not know how it is effected. It may not be out of place to explain it here:

"The opening of every Payment is made on the first day of the month, excepting holy days, for each one of the four annual Payments. During two hours each day set apart for that purpose, is held an assembly of the principal merchants of the place, both French and foreign in the presence of the Provost of merchants, or, in his absence, before the oldest magistrate present, in which assembly commences the acceptance of bills of exchange, payable at the current Payment. This continues till the sixth day of the month inclusive, after which the holders of bills may protest them for non-acceptance during the rest of the month.

"Formerly acceptances were made verbally, and not by writing; but the bankers and merchants of Lyons carried a little book called a Bilan, in which to make acceptances. They entered in it all the bills of exchange drawn upon them, and which were presented by those who were the holders. An acceptance was signified by the mark of a cross on the margin of the book in which they had registered the bills which denoted

8

that the bill was accepted; but if they wished to deliberate whether they would accept the bill or not, they put a letter V. on the margin, which signified (vu, seen) that it had been presented; and when they refused to accept, they put S. P., which signified (sous protest) that it was under protest, that is to say, that the bearer ought to protest it within three days after the current Payment, that is, on or before the third of the following month.

But now acceptances are made in writing, in pursuance of the third article of the law of June, 1667, for reasons which will be mentioned in their place.

" On the third day of the month of Payment, they fixed the rate of exchange between Lyons and all foreign places. This was done at a meeting of merchants, foreign and domestic, in presence of the Provost of merchants.

" On the sixth day, the business of payment commenced, and continued until the last day of the month inclusively, after which no entries in their *bilans*, or book of payments, could be made, and if any were made, they were held to be void according to law.

" The Payments of each day were commenced by the merchant and bearers of *bilans*, in the hall of the exchange at ten o'clock in the morning, and terminated at half past eleven, after which hour no further payment was allowed.

" The mode of proceeding was as follows : The bankers and merchants carried to the exchange their *bilan* of debit and credit; that is to say, a book in which they had written on one side what was due to them, and upon the other, what they owed. They addressed themselves to those to whom they were in debt, and gave them for debtors, one or more of those who owed them a like sum ; this debtor, or debtors being accepted in their place, the substitution was entered in their books, and the debt was regarded as paid. All parties did the same, and so the payments proceeded. At the end of the month, those who owed more than was due to them paid the amount in ready money to the holders of bills who had more coming to them than they owed.

" The bills of exchange payable at the Payment, and not paid before the last day of the month inclusively, were to be protested within the three first days of the following month.

If a banker or merchant accustomed to carry a book at the

place of payment meets with no one willing to accept him as a debtor, during the time of payment, he is reported to have failed. There is no place in the world where merchants are more ready to give credit than at Lyons; so, also, there is no place, where payments are more punctually made; for, if the time of payment is permitted to pass one day, the credit of the party is lost, and he is accounted as bankrupt." Parfait Negociant, par L. Savary, 4to. 1777. tome I. Chap. XII. p. 257.

We have quoted this article on fairs at some length for the purpose of showing that the great operations of commerce were, at the time the Bank of England was established, and when it commenced issuing bank-paper, adjusted by balancing accounts without the use of coin, and that the Bank by issuing paper, based upon these commercial securities, and not upon gold and silver coin, or bullion, only changed the form of balancing the accounts between the respective parties to these dealings; that there is not therefore any honest pretence in claiming, that bank-paper depends upon either of these metals for their efficiency in the making of exchanges and payments.

The coin and bullion which figures so largely in the bank-reports is not for the redemption of bank-bills, but to be sold as a commodity for the settlement of balances, and owned by the parties depositing it.

The bank-credits and its paper was merely another mode of balancing the accounts between commercial dealers in these various exchanges, which had been in use for a great length of time.

If A. had £10,000 to pay in any given month he might have promissory notes, and bills of exchange to the amount of £15,000, due at sixty days, and yet not be able to pay a single pound of his indebtedness. By depositing his securities with the bank, a credit was entered on the bank's book for the paper not due, and upon which credit he was permitted to draw for the amount of each of his liabilities as they became due, and thus to extinguish each debt. So far as A. had claims upon others, which could be balanced through the bank-credit by other claims on A., there was a mutuality which required no money, coin, or bullion to adjust the payments, no matter how many millions were to be adjusted. And as between individuals, so between nations no money is required to make payments, except to pay balances.

When, therefore, the Bank of England, undertook for the mere purposes of gain, to attract business by issuing bank-paper, and giving credits in account, for individual notes not due on demand, it opened a Pandora-box of evils to the business-world, which will never cease until the whole system is extinguished.

The injury inflicted by the system are two-fold, the losses occasioned by it, and the more grave injury—a false education of the people in the belief, that bank-bills owe their value, and efficiency, to coin and bullion the bank never owned, and which for the purposes claimed, never existed. The former robs them, the latter perverts their knowledge, and thereby perpetuates the robbery.

Having unfolded the falsity, and the iniquity of this bank-gold-base-theory in principle some further statistical details of its practical workings, as gathered from its history, will now be given in illustration of the correctness of the views here presented.

It has already been shown, that there was a general crash, or as it is technically denominated, a financial crisis, in 1696, in which the government and bank-securities were badly discredited —to relieve the Bank from insolvency, it was permitted to absorb the indebtedness of the state and the bank into an increase of its capital stock. What the government had eaten up, and consumed in war, or lust of power, re-appeared in the ghostly form of a poverty-producing and labor-consuming interest-bond, and paper-money based on that bond.

In 1708, there was another addition to the bank-stock whereby the power of the Bank was largely increased, and a re-occurrence of the financial difficulties similar to those of '96 avoided. Between 1708 and 1727, in a similar manner and for similar purposes, the bank-capital, was again increased to near £9,000,000. In 1745, another financial "crisis" occurred, which led to a severe run upon the bank; in order to gain time, by amusing the public until the Bank could effect measures to avert an exposure of its insolvent condition by the run, the directors adopted the bank-device usually resorted to, by these fraudulent institutions, of paying in shillings and six-pences until finally it succeeded in allaying the panic, by the more substantial stool-pigeon bank-device of getting the "principal business men," (bank-agents) to subscribe a resolution " declaring their willingness to receive bank-notes in payment of any sum that might be due them, and pledging themselves to use their utmost endeavors to make all their payments in the same medium. Of course the notes of the business men being the only property and security for the bank-notes—the latter would be a good fund for the payment of these business-notes to the Bank. It required therefore no great sacrifice to fool the public, by this *business* resolution of the *business* men. Having succeeded in this, occasion was offered to increase once more the capital stock, which was accordingly improved, by raising it to £10,780,000.

In this connection, we must not omit to mention another important *gold-base* device resorted to by the stockholders and officers of the Bank, to give it credit, in the early period of its history; and that was, to make checks for gold, and obtain parties not in the secret, to draw the gold, in order to give the bank officers an opportunity to make a full display of their immense treasures. The gold was immediately returned to the Bank by the drawee; to be again used for a like purpose. This of course, soon added to the *credit* of the Bank, though like the other *gold-base*, it did not add much value to its bills, nor honest credit to the system.

In 1780, there was another financial "crisis," and in 1762, the capital stock was increased eight per cent., or to £11,642,400. The business of the country revived, and in 1793, the usual bank-accompaniment, "a revulsion was on hand; this continued for two or three years, and as a prelude to the general crisis of 1697, when by an order of Council, dated Sunday, February 26, 1797, the Directors were prohibited from paying their notes in cash, until the sense of Parliament should be taken on the subject. Parliament met, and agreed to continue the restriction till six months after the signature of a definitive treaty of peace.

This suspension of specie-payments, however, was from time to time continued up to 1823, twenty-five full years from its commencement.

In 1814, '15 and '16, there was a continual panic and crash, and in 1816, the payments of what had been consumed in war, was again revived in bonds, and the capital stock of the Bank was raised to £14,453,000, but in 1825 and '26, and again in '35 and '36, in '39, 45, '47, '57, and, 1865, were periods of revulsion, financial disaster and ruin.

In 1844, the British Parliament from its instinctive desire of regulating everything, passed an Act to Regulate the Issue of bank-notes, and for giving to the Governor and Company of the Bank of England, certain privileges for a limited period. "It enacts that from and after the 31st of August, 1844, the issue department of the Bank of England shall be separated from the Banking department; that the issuing department may issue notes to the extent of £14,000,000, upon securities set apart for that purpose, of which the debt of £11,010,100, due from the government to the bank shall form a part; that no amount of notes above £14,000,000 shall be issued, except against gold coin, or gold or silver bullion, and that the silver bullion, shall not exceed one-fourth the amount of gold coin and bullion. Any person is entitled to demand-notes from the issuing department, in exchange for gold bullion, at the rate of £3, 17s., 9d. per ounce. Should any banker discontinue his issue of notes, the Bank of England may, upon application, be empowered by an order of Council to increase her issue upon securities to the extent of two-thirds of the issue thus withdrawn; but all the profit of this increased issue must go to the government."

This act was passed by Parliament to remedy the supposed evils of an inflated currency, under the insane idea that an issue of bank-paper upon a deposit of coin or bullion, for any amount above £14,000,000, the coin would of course redeem the paper, and thereby save the inflation, it probably having never entered the heads of the statesmen who framed, nor of the Parliament which passed that famous Act, that the remedy furnished, only increased the malady.

It will readily be perceived, that the increased issue provided for by this act, while it increased the bank-paper-facilities of trade; it withdrew from circulation, a corresponding amount of coin and bullion. If then this bank-paper, in the prosperous condition of commerce, which its advent would be likely to furnish, should stimulate an excess of importations to the amount, say £15,000,000 above what the annual productive industry, through the ordinary channels of business would be able to supply, what then, would be the beneficial results secured by the Act? We answer: none whatever, but on the contrary, the coin and bullion, upon which the bills had been issued, must now be had to settle balances of the foreign trade. This would occasion a corresponding and sudden withdrawal of the bank-bills from circulation which would soon precipitate a financial revulsion, ruinous to every branch of domestic industry and trade.

While the Regulation of the issue of bank-notes, upon the favorite gold-base theory of the British statesmen succeeded, it did not succeed in annulling the great fundamental laws which govern the production and distribution of property, though it set them at defiance. Hence during the last twenty-five years since the passage of that Act, no less than four severe revulsions have visited the British Isles.

The revulsion of 1847, was one of the most severe which has ever occurred in that country—the failures in London and Liverpool alone, in less than sixty days exceeded £41,000,000, the total loss estimated in the United States money of account was, $37,774,500. If these losses from financial revulsions, since, and including that of 1797, have been as severe on an average, as that of 1847, they will exceed $200,000,000.

There is one peculiarity in this British national debt and bank legislation, which is now attempted on a large scale, to be re-enacted over again in this country, and which must not be overlooked ; and that is, that while the labor, and the business of the country based on that labor, outside of the Bank, furnishes nine-tenths of all the means for the support of the government, and for the present and future redemption of the bank-notes and credits issued, and granted by the Bank, yet, whenever the annual industry of the country fails to supply the exorbitant demands of the government, and the bank excesses, the deficit is sure to be made up by an increased supply of Bank capital, and of interest bearing national bonds.

By this bank and bond system, a man must be taxed when he is born, for being born, and while he lives, he is taxed because he lives, and when he dies, because he dies, and if he is so unfortunate as to have an estate, his estate is taxed, because in taxing the owner out of existence, his estate was not all absorbed into the hands of the Bankocracy during its owners life-time.

Besides the use of individual capital, which the Bank has to sustain it, there is a constant stream of public revenues all the while pouring into the Treasury by taxation ; these funds vary in the amount kept on hand, from two to twelve millions pounds sterling. On the 17th December, 1852, the Government deposits were, £10,492,686.

If anything more is needed to show the utter falsity and

rottenness of this gold-base and coin-redemption bank-theory, it can be best furnished in the monthly and annual Reports of the Bank. The following is an example: February 28th, 1798, circulation, £16,095,830; deposits, £6,148,900; securities, £16,799,500; bullion, £5,828,940; surplus, £3,385,710. February 28th, 1815, circulation, £27,261,650; deposits, £11,702,250; securities, £44,558,501; bullion, £2,036,910; surplus, £7,631,510. February 23d, 4841, circulation, £16,399,000; deposits, £6,407,000; securities, £21,344,000; bullion, £4,335,000; surplus, £2,873,000. February 28th, 1824, circulation, £19,736,990; deposits, £10,097,850; securities, £18,872,000; bullion, ££13,810,060: surplus £2,847,226.

In all these returns it will be seen that the circulation and deposits very largely exceed the bullion and coin, while that of 1815 shows an excess of £36,927,990, or in the United States money of account, $184,639,950, due to the public, over all its bullion and coin.

The gold-base, and the gold convertible theory of the Bank of England, is a myth which never had an existence anywhere, but in the muddled brains of the British public, and those of other nations, who have been unwise and wicked enough, to follow in her wake.

But by this double device, England has robbed her industrial classes of their annual earnings, until about one-eighth of her population are paupers. And by the capital thus accumulated, and the adoption of her gold-theories, she has been enabled to derange the industries of the civilized world; to make nations pay her a tribute, of all they possess, and at her bidding to bow down and worship her GOLDEN CALF.

CHAPTER X.

THE BANKS OF SCOTLAND.

The banking system of Scotland is the best which has yet been devised. It presents a contrast compared with the English system as distinct, and marked, as can well be imagined. As its origin was different, so has been its subsequent history. The Bank of England was instituted as a great engine of state, for the centralization of power. What would benefit the ruling classes was duly considered; that which related to the interest of the governed, received no further attention than was necessary to subserve the purposes of the governmental class. It commenced its career, with a loan of all its funds, to the government; and from that day, to the present, its course has been a continual round of the most grasping, overreaching acts of despotism, and fraud, upon the rights of the governed, which the world's history has furnished. Every great misfortune and loss of the industrial classes, whether by war, famine, or pestilence, has been the occasion for an increase of its power. What was lost or consumed of the people's earnings in war, as has been shown, re-appeared in a two-fold form of interest to continue to eat out the people's substance for the benefit of the governmental class. But not so the Scotch system. The Scotch banks were created to subserve the interests of commerce. Its active promoters and founders were commercial men, who were well acquainted with the practical operations of trade, and knew full well, that the great transactions of commerce were carried on, not by gold, or silver, but by credit. That to settle a balance the avails of £1000 of tea which was in the trade, was as good, and even better, than £1000 of gold, which was not in the trade, and which neither the merchant, nor banker, had. These men too, were well acquainted with the history of conducting business and making payments, at the great fairs, which at that time occupied so prominent a place in the business of the European world. They also understood that the institution of the banks of Venice, Genoa, Amsterdam, and Hamburg was to get rid of using either coin or bullion, for any other purpose in trade, but that of a commodity in settling balances.

The Bank of Scotland owes its origin to the efforts of John Holland, a merchant of London. Its charter was granted by the Scotch Parliament, in 1695, (Will. III. Part 1, § 5.) "Its original capital was £1,200,000 Scotch, or £100,000 Sterling, distributed in shares of £1000 Scotch, or £83, 6s, 8d Sterling, each."

The Act exempted the capital from all public burdens, and gave it the exclusive privilege of banking in Scotland for 21 years. The responsibility of the shareholders is limited to the amount of their shares. The capital of the Bank was increased to £200,000 in 1744, and in 1804, to £1,500,000.

The Bank of Scotland is the only Scotch Bank constituted by Act of Parliament. It established branches in 1696, and issued notes for one pound as early as 1704.

Holland, and some merchants in London and Edinburgh, who disliked the Bank of England, upon an assurance from the Scotch Government, that such an Act as was desired, could be had, drew up a plan. Holland has given an account of his connection with the Institution of the Bank, in a pamphlet bearing this ominous title: "The Ruine of the Bank of England, and all public credit inevitable." Holland, as a merchant, knowing the practical modes of exchange, had no faith in the effect of legislative enactments. He was probably acting under the delusive idea that this was an attempt to establish by force of mere legislative enactment, a money without any regard to the powers granted, as applicable to the natural uses, to which these legal powers were applicable.

No nation it is believed, however despotic its power, has ever been able by mere arbitrary enactment to maintain for any considerable length of time the circulation of a money thus instituted, at anything like par.

A legal tender is useful to the full extent to which it can be made practically to operate. If there are public taxes to be paid so far as that demand operates, an issue of paper not exceeding the amount required for the payment of such taxes, would be at or near par. So of exchanges, the issue of all the money which is needed to make the exchanges of one useful article for another, without being obliged to transport any article in any other manner than what the natural demand for that article for consumption requires, would keep the money, at or near par, from its legal and commercial uses in making payments, although of no appreciable, actual or intrinsic value.

Holland, viewing the provision to loan the money to the government as subversive of the legitimate purposes of instituting a money for commercial uses, was justly suspicious of the power, and so much so, that he overlooked the great fact, that this bank charter contained all the powers necessary to enable the Bank to furnish the facilities of a circulating medium, that was contained in the Scotch Bank Charter of Holland and others. In addition to this, the government made it a depository of her power, in the bond interest capital, and by the constant revenues of the government. The injury, therefore, which was likely to flow from instituting the Bank of England, did not lie in the direction of ruining the credit of the nation, but in the immense grant of powers and thereby the control and absorption of too large a portion of the annual productive industry of the country, in interest and taxes, and such has been the result. All the vast revenues of the nation are poured into the Bank Treasury, without stint or measure, and through this organized over-taxation, and double interest, the industrial classes of the nation are perpetually robbed, and financial revulsions every few years, with all their attendant evils, follow in their train.

But Holland and his associates, taking the view above suggested, were determined that the Scotch Bank should not be ruined by loaning money to either kings, or government, had a prohibition against it inserted in their charter. Thus originated the diverse character and practices of the two institutions—the English Bank Charter was granted on condition of loaning the government £1,200,000 for twelve years, and the Scotch Charter was allowed its monopoly for twenty-one years, without any concessions, or paying any bonus to the government. The former therefore, relied upon its concentrated governmental powers and perquisites for its success—the latter upon conciliating the industrial and business public by advantages offered.

From these ever-diverging stand-points of government and motive-power incorporated into these two charters, at the beginning—the Bank of England has succeeded in establishing a bank-governmental power, which has effectually crushed out the rights and liberties of the people—the Bank of Scotland, as before stated, in establishing the best banking-system yet devised.

The Bank of Scotland started with the design of making credits, based on property, as contra-distinguished from coin, or bullion, answer as far as possible all demands of business in making an exchange. Hence it early issued bank-notes, from £100 down to £1, and less. It sought to identify itself with the people, not in seeking patronage of the government, or of a special class.

The laborer who deposited his £5, stood side by side with the merchant and the capitalist. The Bank paid one per cent. less, than the current rate of interest, on its deposits, and faithfully returned them on demand.

This system has secured these savings for business purposes, in place of seeking investment (as in financial language it is popularly denominated) in public stocks, or to be loaned on bonds and mortgages. The poor feel the same interest in the safe management of the Bank, as do their more wealthy neighbors. Industry, prudence and thrift, have been promoted by the line of business thus early adopted by the bank. The hatred and jealousy of Banks in England, and the United States, finds no place among the Scotch people. Universal confidence in the soundness of their system, pervades all classes of society. This feeling of security no doubt, is very largely attributable to the liberal policy inaugurated by the Bank of Scotland.

There are forty banks which have established 340 branch offices. These banks are not the rival establishments, like the English, of a conflicting system striving for supremacy, but are parts of a harmonious whole. Hence, in no other country is there a currency so free from fluctuations in quantity, and so uniformly good, as that of Scotland.

English statesmen with their characteristic itching propensity for a centralized despotism, have been seeking for more than a century, for some excuse to engraft upon the Scotch system, that "sum of all villanies" the English *gold-base*; but the Scotch with equal tenacity cling to their own superior system, without the "gold-base."

The English cannot understand the Scotch system, but the Scotch do understand the English, and its grossly fraudulent and despotic base. They have witnessed the terrible judgments visited upon England in the form of revulsions for the impious worship of their dagon of gold; from all which, Scotland has been almost entirely exempt. This intermeddling disposition of English statesmen, to disturb, or displace the Scotch system by their own, meets with the scorn and contempt of the Scotch, which it so richly deserves, and they do not fail to remind the English that their system cannot be depended upon at home.

This contest in Parliament, and out of it, has been long and bitter; but the Scotch thus far, have come off victorious. Sir Walter Scott compares these intermeddling efforts of the English, to an eccentric, but hospitable Scotch laird, who forced every guest who sojourned with him, to follow his practice of taking every night one of Anderson's pills, " only one leetle Anderson," of the British Government. It would be well for the American people if Congress could be induced to stop feeding " leetle Andersons."

But not to digress further, the great efficiency of Scotch banking over the English and American, lies in cash credits in account. This is peculiarly Scotch—it exists nowhere else. It is not the amount of business done through this medium, but it is the system itself, which has such a controlling influence over every other branch of Scottish banking business and labor.

The number of these cash accounts are not far from £5,000,000, and the deposits are £30,000,000. The importance of the cash credits does not consist in the amount, but in the functions they perform, and the order and activity which has been thereby introduced into the channels of business.

The following outline of the system will explain its uses: The Bank opens an account with a customer from £100 to £1000, which is at his disposal or use, but not placed to his credit. The Bank is secured against loss by a bond. But the present redemption, or the integrity of the credit depends upon the avails of the property purchased from day to day. Hence the business qualification, pecuniary ability, and the character of the business are essential elements in determining the propriety, or impropriety of opening an account. The following is the form of the bond used.

" We, A. B., C. D. and E. F., considering, that the Bank has agreed to allow us a standing credit to the extent of one thousand pounds sterling, upon a cash credit account, to be kept in the name of one of us, the said A. B., in the books of the said Bank, and to be operated upon by him, and may also discount or purchase bills, whereon the name of the said A. B., or the firm of any company of which he is a partner, may stand as a drawer, acceptor or indorser, and that upon condition of our granting these presents: *Therefore*, we, the said A. B., C. D. and E. F., hereby bind and oblige ourselves, as full debtors and co-obligants, and our respective heirs, executors, and successsors, and successors whomsoever, all conjointly and severally, to content and pay to the said part or parts thereof as the said A. B., or any person or persons having his letter or other written authority, shall value for, or draw out by orders or drafts on the said Bank, or its manager, cashier, or any of its officers at Edinburgh, or of any of its agents, cashiers, or other officers elsewhere, in virtue of the foresaid credit; and also such sum or sums of money, as the said A. B. shall stand engaged for, or be indebted, resting or owing to the said Bank, on account of any bills discounted or held by it, whereon his name as an individual, or the firm of any company of which he is a partner, shall stand as drawer, acceptor, or endorser, or any sum or sums for which he, or they shall stand engaged, or indebted to the said Bank, by acceptances, endorsations, letters of credits, guarrantees, or in any other manner of way whatsoever, and all or any of which obligations, as aforesaid, the said Bank shall be entitled to place to the debit of the said account, and of the obligants hereto, at any time before this bond is discharged and delivered up, and that without intimation to any of the said parties, but not exceeding in all the said principal sum of one thousand pounds sterling, and interest due thereon; and that at any time when the same shall be demanded after three months from the date hereof, together with the legal interest thereof, from the time or times of the respective advances, until the same be repaid, with a fifth part more of the said principal sum due, of penalty in case of failure. And it is hereby specially conditioned and agreed to, that a stated account, made out from the books of said Bank, and signed by one of its accountants, shall be sufficient to constitute a charge or balance against us, except on consignation only of the sum due thereon. And it is hereby declared that there is nothing hereby meant to supersede or vacate the security, which the said Bank already holds, or may hold over any shares of stock of the said Bank and profits thereon, belonging or that may belong to any of us for any advances under this bond or otherwise; it being always in the power of the said

Bank to appropriate or allow of the disposal in any way whatever of all or any of the shares of said stock, and the said parties to this bond hereby declare that they have no lien over the said shares, or any right to insist upon the application of the same to payment of any debts to be hereby contracted. And further, the said parties agree that the obligation hereby comes under, shall remain in full force in the same manner, and to the same extent, as if such shares of stock had never belonged to any of the parties' hereto, and it being hereby agreed that the said Bank may allow credit on the said shares, or the same to be sold, and the price to be paid to the seller, or may apply the same to any other purpose, according as it shall deem expedient, being bound in the latter case to account only to' the person or persons to whom the shares belonged.

"And further declaring, as the said cash credit account is to be in the name of the said A. B., and he is to conduct the transactions thereon, it is hereby especially provided and agreed to, that all communications on the part of the Bank, regarding either the management by him of the accounts or repayment of the balances, which may become due thereon, shall or may be made to us, the other parties, through the said A. B., with whom the said Bank shall be at liberty to make any arrangement of the accounts according to the rules of the said Bank if deviated from, or in any other way required, or by giving time for repayment of the balance or balances thereof, without any direct application to or concurrence by us, the said C. D. and E. F., on the subject, until the said Bank shall consider this necessary for a final settlement. And it shall also have the power, without any consultation with or consent by us, to compromise with, or give time to any of the parties on the bills discounted or held by it as aforesaid, we, the said C. D. and E. F., having always full opportunity afforded us by the said Bank, whenever we, or either of us, wish and apply for the same, to see any of the transactions and state of the said cash account, and other transactions of the said A. B., in which we may be interested by the obligations of this bond, and the said Bank shall only be bound to attend to any instructions we may give on the subject in writing, and acknowledged in writing to have been received. It being hereby expressly declared that all the parties to this bond are *pari passu* co-obligants to the said Bank; and that all and each of us are equally bound to it, and shall not be entitled to plead that any of us are the cautioners for the other; and we, the said A. B. and E. F., consent to the registration hereof, and of the foresaid stated accounts, in the books of council and session, that letters of honoring on six days' charge, and, thereto in form as officers, and for that purpose we constitute, etc.

" In Witness whereof, these presents, written upon this sheet of *stamped* paper, by our procurators."

This cash credit accommodation, is only granted by the directors of the principal Bank, and upon a strict examination of the applicant, as to his business, means and prospects.

The bond as will be seen, covers all liabilities to the Bank, whether as drawer or endorser. There is no limit to the use of the credit—it is terminable at the pleasure of either party. But such a termination seldom occurs, except where parties desire to close business.

This credit is a mutual benefit, the holder of the credit has all the benefit of having the cash on hand to make purchases, without the risk of holding the cash, and the Bank gets its interest for the sum drawn at one per cent. higher rate of interest than it allows the customer for his deposits. The account is balanced when convenient, generally twice a year at least. A credit account under the Scotch system, is a loan of the Bank's credit for present use, and a charge for as much of the credit as is used and no more. Whereas, the English system the credit is virtually a discount—it requires a transfer of the securities to the Bank, and interest upon the whole credit from the moment the transfer is made, whether that credit is used or not. The theory of the English system is, that the credit must be had only upon business already finished up, and to be governed in quantity by the amount done. The theory of the Scotch system is, that men want cash to do business when the business is done, and that the business men having secured them for the ready cash, must have it at such times, and in such amounts, as their business demands, subject only to the supervision of the Bank, that the business fulfills the reasonable requirements of the contract between the Bank and customer. To an English banker that would lead to over-trading; he, like his government and governmental principle, has no faith in the reason and discretion of his customer, further, than he secures him absolutely and unconditionally, and pays a big rate of interest. But the Scotch-man knows by long experience that such fears are groundless

...ს men under the guidance of their judgments and the direct supervision of sureties and the Bank, make the most safe and reliable business men in the world. Under their system there is no one who has a greater interest in conducting the business prudently than the man himself.

The difference then in doing business for one year on a thousand pounds sterling would be this: In England, if a £1000 was provided for, say for ninety days, at 5 per cent., and this arrangement would cost in round numbers, say £50, and whatever securities were pledged, would be in the hands of the Bank and under its control. Whatever money was deposited would have no effect in reducing the interest due to the Bank. But under the Scotch system a customer might from the avails of his business during the year, have an average of deposits, amounting to eight hundred pounds sterling, and if his business demands should require the use of £1000, then his account would stand thus: Use of £1000, one year, £50; interest on deposits, £800, at 4 per cent., £32; cost of the bank credit, £18. On the score of cost then, the Scotch system is much the most favorable, and on the score of a prudent, safe, and uniform business, there is no comparison whatever to be instituted between the two systems—the balance is largely in favor of the Scotch system.

Under both systems, the merchandize purchased, and not gold or silver, furnishes the fund for the redemption of the money, and the amount paid is not strictly interest, or rent, but merely so much is paid for managing the books of their customers, and the risk that the Bank runs of being eventually liable if the parties themselves do not receive enough of their purchases to redeem the banker's money or credit, and to pay him for endorsing it, and keeping an account of the transaction.

The difference in the modes of transacting business between the English and Scotch systems as respects the effects which bear upon the efficiency of the institutions themselves, is in every particular decidedly in favor of the Scotch, being far the most reliable and efficient. To illustrate the practical workings of both modes from the stand-point here presented; let it be supposed that the credit account in each case is £5,000,000, under the English theory this sum is for business already done, and upon the several parties own capital, (which like their bank-money being based on gold, is equally false,)and yet the bank-money is to pay debts then due, and this money is liable to be redeemed, on demand in coin or bullion, while the actual funds for its redemption are bills of exchange and promissory notes, due at from sixty to ninety days after date. It is in this manner that financial pressures are sure to arise. While under the Scottish system this £5,000,000 credit, are only payable in bank-notes. If the holders demand gold, the gold is refused, and the accounts closed. The banks always hold as large a demand in paper against the public as the public do against the banks, and the bank's claims are at home, and payments can be demanded in a few hours, whereas, the claims against them are scattered over the country, and cannot all be made in many days.

The payment of debts in Scotland is not made as in England and the United States, from paper discounted, but by means of these cash credits—these credits are not based upon securities for business done, but is in advance of the business—it leaves it at the option of the owner of the credit to make the purchases upon his own credit upon as long time as he can obtain, and then to pay the avails of the sales in liquidating the debt, drawing the balance from his credits, or he can pay his cash at once, and rely upon his sales to reimburse the Bank, which cannot be done by the English system, as the sales have already been made, and the avails are turned out as collaterals for the security of the money.

Hence, in Scotland, the money is drawn, or provided for in advance, and it keeps up an equal circulation, whereas, in England, a large refusal to discount notes to pay debts already due, may of itself produce a stringency in the money market, and cause a panic from that source.

There is another advantage in the Scotch system, not to be had under the English cash credits—the average amount of money required in the Scotch mode of doing business, will not generally much exceed £3,000,000, on credits of £5,000,000, which takes a much less amount of interest from the customer, and secures thereby the solvency and prompt payment of the cash credit.

A witness testified before Parliament, in an examination made in 1826: "I have hardly ever heard of a bad debt by cash accounts. The Bank of Scotland, I am sure, lost hardly anything in an amount of receipts and payments of hundreds of millions. They may have lost a few hundred pounds in a century."

In 1797, when the Bank of England had to take shelter behind an order of the Privy Council and Acts of Parliament, to exempt it from the demands for specie—there was no demand for specie by the Scotch Banks, nor was there any demand or any order for their relief. In the Report of a Select Committee, made to the House of Lords, in 1826, they say: "It is proved by the evidence and by the documents, that the Banks of Scotland, whether chartered joint-stock companies, or private establishments, have for more than a century exhibited a stability, which the committee believe to be unexampled in the history of banking, that they supported themselves, from 1797 to 1812, without any protection from the restriction by which the Bank of England, and that of Ireland, were relieved from cash payments; that there was little demand for gold during the late embarrassments in the circulation, [in 1825–'26], and that, in the whole period of their establishment, there are not more than two or three instances of bankruptcy, as, during the whole of this period, a large portion of their issues consisted almost entirely of notes not exceeding £1, or £1 1s., there is the strongest reason for concluding that, as far as respects the Banks of Scotland, the issue of paper of that denomination has been found compatible with the highest degree of solidity; and that there is not therefore, while they are conducted on the present system, sufficient ground for proposing any alteration, with a view of adding to a solidity which has so long been sufficiently established."

Sir Robert Peel, was Chairman of a Committee of the House of Commons, appointed the same year, to ascertain, whether the Act limiting the issue of bank-notes to denominations not less than £5 notes, should be extended to Scotland, Reports—that they "cannot advise that a law should now be passed, prohibiting from a period to be herein determined the future issue in Scotland of notes under £5," and that they are "unwilling without stronger proof of necessity, to incur the risks of deranging, from any cause whatever, a system admirably calculated in their opinion, to economize the use of capital, to excite and cherish a spirit of useful enterprise, and even to promote the moral habits of the people, by the direct inducements it holds out to the maintenance of a character for industry, integrity and prudence."

The merits of the Scotch system and its management, must have been admirable to have elicited such commendation from English statesmen. Yet, with England it is not a question of soundness, as a reliable medium of exchange, but one of power. For nearly two hundred years her statesmen have been gradually loosening their hold on feudalism, and substituting an organized system of corporations, to grind out the rights, and the annual productions of her industrial classes. The lords of manors may die, but the lords of soulless corporations never. By this subtle system, the centre of which is her bank-power, England has not only pauperized her labor-population, and flooded the now world, with her rich crops of paupers and criminals, but by inducing other nations to adopt her gold-base theories, and especially new countries who have not such a centralization of wealth and power. She is enabled to derange their manufacturing industries, to keep their labor-populations in the semi-barbarous practice, of exhausting their soils, to furnish the raw materials for British manufacturers to manufacture, and food to feed, her pauper operatives.

The adoption then of England's gold-base theory by other nations, and an aping of the policy, without her centralization of wealth and power, enables her to rule the world—not by laws, but by policies. London is thus made the world's government seat. In it governments and peoples are merchandize. Public rights and public interest are bound up in bonds and stocks. Nations' industries and nations rights are hawked out on terms of sale, fixed by London stock-jobbers and gold-gamblers. Here every stock-jobbing establishment is furnished for this purpose with an annual revised edition of every bond and stock, national, state, or corporate. At the head of this gambling list of stocks, stands the United States. Her national, state, railroad, canal, and other corporate stocks with the laws, dates of issuing, and time of payment, are all duly noted, and set forth, with an accuracy, and fulness of detail, never dreamed of in any official Report for the people of the United States, and these Reports are furnished by government-bond, railroad, and other corporate officials, for the special use of these London stock-jobbers.

If the industrial classes of this country desire to know the manner, and the place, where labor, laborers and their rights, are hawked out as a thing of little worth, let them study the system by which it is done, and a full exhibit of the details can be found in a list of the London stock board, if this is not satisfactory, consult its echo in this country, the New York stockboard. This lesson if thoroughly studied and well understood, will disclose the important fact, that a nations liberties, and its industrial interests, are not wrapt up in flaming declarations of rights, whether in pronunciamentos or bills of rights, but their subversion is contained in the great fundamental laws, financial and corporate.

From an attentive examination of this subject too, it is easy to discover the reason why English statesmen, periodically, every few years, make a systematic attack upon the Scotch banking system. It is not because the Scotch system is not a good one. It is not because they are afraid Scotch £1 notes may circulate on the other side of the Tweed—nor is it even a periodical fit of gold-base spleen.—but it is purely a question of power. English statesmen very well understand that the world's intermeddlers and liberty-haters, owe their supremacy, not to having the strongest battalions, but by having the most centralized and despotic money-power, which ever scourged a nation, or cursed the earth.

If Scotland had the natural resources of the United States, and it was necessary to interfere with her annual industries to gather them into British granaries and vaults, her superior banking-system would not be permitted to stand in the way of British greed and lust of power, for a single moment. As the English revenue system gathers all that can safely be extorted from the Scotch, an officious intermeddling with the Scottish modes of exchange, would be more disastrous to English interest, if possible, than her misrule in Ireland. Scotch tenacity, backed by such considerations as these; has enabled her thus far to slip through the English governmental iron fingers.

If this English gold-base and reformatory bank-zeal run in the direction of justice, and the welfare of subjects, instead of the perpetuation of a despotism over them, then Scotland's banking history is bristling on every side with facts which give a flat denial to all of England's despotic and lying gold-base theories.

Neither the rebellion, 1715, nor that of 1745, nor the disturbances following the French Revolution of 1793, or that of 1797 nor even the great crash of 1825, were able to disturb the Scotch system, or induce the people to make a run upon their banks. While the Bank of England, in all these disturbances was most seriously pressed; in 1797, she suspended payments in coin, and continued that suspension for twenty-five years.

"In Scotland," says Colwell, in his late treatise, p. 427 "they understand as well as they do in England, the use of gold "—they know its value as a commodity, (especially under coinage and mint regulations,) but being a costly commodity, they do not incline to use it as a currency, except so far as their bank currency fails of its object; nor do they wish to purchase or hold it as commodity, except for such special purpose as may promise adequate advantage. Their system of banking enables them to dispense with it almost entirely. In this they are far from thinking themselves behind their neighbors in intelligence or financial skill."

Sir Walter Scott, in referring to the oft-repeated metaphor that gold, like water will find its level—Says : "A metaphor is no argument in any instance, but I think I can contrive in the present, to turn this water-engine against those who employ it. Scotland, sir, is not beneath that level, and she may perish for want of it, ere she sees a guinea, without she, or the state for her, be at the perpetual expense of maintaining, by constant expenditure, that metallic currency which has a natural tendency to escape from a poor country back to a rich one." " In countries where gold is indispensible, it must be obtained, whatever price is given for it, while the means of paying such a price remains."

" If my friend would consult the clerk of the Water Company, at his office in the Royal Exchange, [Edinburgh], he would explain the matter at once. 'Let me have,' says Mr. Chrystal, ' a pipe of water to my house.' 'Certainly sir, it will cost you forty shillings yearly.' 'The devil it will?' 'Why, surely the Lawnmarket is lower than the Reservoir on the Castle Hill ?' 'It is the nature of the water to come to a level. What title have you to charge me money, when the element is only obeying the laws of nature and descending to its level ?' 'Very true sir,' replies the clerk, 'but then it was no law of nature brought it to the Reservoir, at a height which was necessary to enable us to disperse the supply over the city. On the contrary it was an exertion of art, in despite of nature. It was forced hither by much labor and ingenuity. Lakes were formed, aquaducts constructed, rivers dammed up, and pipes laid for many miles. Without immense expense, the water could never have been brought here; and without your paying a rateable charge you cannot have the benefit of it.

Scotland according to Sir Walter Scott's views, did not employ a gold currency because it had to be purchased and paid for; and she had no inducement to make so expensive a purchase, in the face of the fact which long experience had taught her that she could do better without it; that her people preferred the bank-paper to gold. The views of Sir Walter Scott, in his celebrated pamphlet, were emphatically seconded by his country-men of every class, and they retained their well-tried paper system, which though convertible by law as in England is so wisely adjusted that a run upon banks for gold or silver, is an event which has not occurred for a century in Scotland.

The position occupied by banks in England and Scotland, in the eyes of the people are widely different. In England, the people are taught to look to the test of convertibility of liabili-ties into gold, or payment on demand, as the only right criterion of the solvency of the banks; they well know nevertheless, that this convertibility is not possible, and never was. Every bank is regarded as having undertaken what if called upon it could not perform; and every man is left to his own discretion about the degree of forbearance he can safely exercise. In times of commercial prosperity, the distrust which this view of the banks generates, in a greater or less degree, in all minds may be latent and unseen; but the moment any cause of alarm arises, this dis-trust is aroused to fearful energy and action. Every man's appre-hensions are multiplied by his estimate of other people's fears, and in England, as well as the United States, a run upon the banks is inevitable in a time of commercial derangements, or disturbance. When the banks sustain themselves upon such occasions, it is often regarded as triumphant proof of their solidity and strength, though the merciless process by which the banks defend themselves, by contracting the currency, has inflicted losses upon individuals to, many times the amount of the coin in the banks. Under the English system, every attack upon the banks is inevitably attended by an attack of the banks upon their customers, and through them upon the whole com-munity. To save a million of gold lying unemployed in their vaults, the banks will diminish the active paper currency, two, or three, or even ten millions. The banks of England are looked upon then, by the people, as institutions exposed to great risk, and as capable in times of commercial trouble, of inflicting terrible losses upon the community in which they are placed; they are isolated, each is standing upon its own strength, and frequently as prompt to sacrifice each other in averting the dreaded suspension, as to fall upon their customers by the process of contraction. In England and the United States, an unappeasable jealousy of banks pervades a large portion of the people, which requires little special provocation to rouse into active enmity and opposition.

In Scotland there is no jealousy of the banks; they are not hated as monopolists nor distrusted as unsafe. They stand together as one mass, prepared to uphold each other in every danger, and to sustain their customers in time of trial. The contractions of currency which in England prove such a. severe scourge, the power of employing which the banks there regard as one of their most important privileges are unknown in Scotland.

The Scottish banks have from their commencement received deposits as low as £10, and some even less, upon which they paid interest at about one per cent. less than the current rate. The deposits thus made for the sake of accumulation, ranging from £10 upwards, have for a long period exceeded ten millions sterling, perhaps they now exceed fifteen. There is the interest which the masses have in the banks of Scotland. The confidence of these depositors is so great, that since the introduction of saving's banks in Scotland, the poor commence their savings in them by shillings, and continue their economy, until they have succeeded in accumulating £10, which they carry to a bank for a regular deposit receipt. The Scotch banks are the pride of the people, all their spare money is at interest in them, and, never hearing the language of distrust or opposition, no fear or apprehension crosses their minds. No one has ever heard of a difficulty in collecting either principal or interest, or in re-investing them together. The people know that all the notes of all the banks are good over all Scotland, and that if a suspicion were raised against any one bank, the others would make a point of giving their own notes for those suspected. It would be difficult to find a man in Scotland in whom a doubt existed, or could be planted of the entire soundness of all their banks, now and hereafter. The system of redemption semi-weekly between all the banks, and their many local exchanges, give them such an oversight of their respective operations, that they have less fear of each other's solvency than the isolated banks of England. The banks of Scotland, consisting mainly of branches of a small number of banks situated in the chief towns, are governed by a policy which is uniform, and equally designed for the benefit of the whole people and the safety of the banks. This *esprit du corps*, which prevails among the banks of Scotland, has been strongly censured in England as likely to lead to over-issues relying on mutual aid ; but it must be noted that there is among the banks there, not only a disposition to protect each other in danger, but an equally strong tendency to watch each other at all times. Their respective interests demand this, and their close association makes this watchfulness effective. Whilst all, therefore are disposed to help each one that may need aid, all are equally interested to restrain the tendency of any one to go astray.

The comparative success of the Scottish banking system during a century and half. While it commands the admiration of those who study it with proper attention, does not always convince them that it could with equal advantage, be transplanted in another soil. It might be long before that confidence in banks, which exists in Scotland, could be inspired elsewhere. A popular writer referring to this, says : The credit of one establishment might be doubted for the time—that of the general system was never brought into question. Even avarice, the most suspicious of passions, has in no instance I ever heard of, desired to compose her hands by an accumulation of the precious metals. The confidence in the credit of our ordinary medium has not been doubted, even in the dreams of the most veritable and jealous of human passions. If this extraordinary faith in bank currency is of long growth in Scotland, and therefore not transferable elsewhere, there must at least be something in the system which promoted that steady growth, and which headed off all those accidents and commercial troubles which elsewhere have not only destroyed confidence in banks, but through them inflicted incalculable mischief upon the people. It is in this aspect, that the history, constitution and practice of the Scottish banks has not been properly studied out of Scotland nor even in it. The value of the system is fully appreciated at home, but no Scottish writer has yet shown what elements in the system have given it such a large and firm growth.

We refer to one peculiarity in Scotland, without, however, looking for its origin; it is fixed in the minds of the Scottish people, that whatever will fully perform the functions of money, in purchase and payments, is as good as money for them, and, if cheaper and more convenient, it is to be preferred and employed. Such a substitute they find their bank-currency to be. They see and know that it does not perform these functions in virtue of its being convertible, but that it answers the end designed like a steam-engine, because it is properly devised for the purpose. They know that men pay their debts by balancing their books of account, and that the debts so paid are well and fully paid, and they know equally well, that the debts paid by the agency of their bank-notes are also fully and properly discharged. They know that, in all this, there is no intervention of money or the precious metals. In Scotland, they look, therefore, upon coined money as a thing to be obtained and employed when there is need for it. They are so satisfied with their present modes of payment, that they have no more desire of replacing their one pound notes with sovereigns, than a man of business has to wear buttons of gold, or to drink from vessels of gold, because it is a substance of real value. In Scotland the people have no fear of the banking-system breaking down, they can see no possibility of that, so long as they continue their confidence. They do not regard it as resting upon gold; and if the directors of the Scottish banks were to send their whole stock of gold to London, reserving only what might be needful for change and the supply of travellers to England, it would create no panic, no run. They know that their banking-system is a device to effect payments in their business. Those who have bank-notes are sure that they can at any time buy as much gold as they may require, but they no more think of turning their bank-notes into gold, unless it is needed for a particular purpose, than of turning them into precious stones. Such is the long and deeply settled feeling and opinion of the Scottish people; and it is no doubt due to some element in their system, the influence of which has not yet been sufficiently understood."

The vast superiority of the Scotch banking-system over the English, and the strong attachment of the Scotch to it, will be found to lie in the fact that it is an honest system, well administered, based on a true theory as far as any system can be, probably, where the power of the government is let out for private gain.

Its soundness as well as cheapness may be illustrated by the following example A. has a hundred loaves of bread, the avails of which he desires to put into a pair of boots, he sells the bread to B. for $6.00, who having a cash credit at the bank, draws a check, and pays A. B. retains two loaves as profit, and sells the balance to C., but C. having neither money, nor cash credit, gives to B. his note for ninety days at five per cent. interest, and C. in like manner takes out his two loaves profit and sells to D. for $6.00, and the bread thus passes down through the whole alphabet to Z., who buys the fifty loaves and pays $6.00, the amount received from A. for a pair of boots. Z. pays this $6.00 to Y., and in a reversed order each party settling the interest, it passes back to B. who balances the cash credit in the transaction. In the mean time B. has been constantly making deposits, so that his account would stand thus: he has drawn out $6.00, and has had an average of $4.00 on deposit. B. therefore, for three months pays 5 per cent. interest for $6.00, and is allowed four per cent. interest on $4.00, or he pays the bank 7½ cents, and receives four cents credit. The bank accommodation under the Scotch system would have cost 3½ cents, on $6.00 for ninety days. Under the English it would be thirty cents—a difference of 14 cents, or the Scotch would be two and one-third per cent. per annum interest, where the English would be five per cent. This demonstrates that the Scotch system is much the most economical, and it would be difficult to conceive, how gold or silver could have added anything to the efficiency of these exchanges, or to the value of the money, if it could not, then coin would have been a useless expense. But the English claim that as coin and bullion are used in settling balances, that every paper dollar requires a gold or silver dollar in the bank vault, that no paper-money can be sound, which does not virtually rest on such a coin or bullion base. It is very well understood, however, that no paper-money ever had such a base in fact, that ninety-nine dollars out of every hundred of business done, is by paper money, or credit, without any reference whatever to either coin or bullion. British statesmen and savans have therefore sagely concluded that a safe paper-money system requires, that there should be idle, in the vaults of the bank, coin and bullion to the amount of at least one-third of the paper-issue. This deposit is not used for the purpose of redeeming the bank-money, to any considerable extent, but principally to settle balances in the foreign trade. Hence it is claimed, that the circulation should fluctuate with the demand for coin and bullion, and not with the demands for the property exchanged, which is the actual base of the money. If therefore the natural demand for money among the people to exchange their products were £500,000,000, including bank-notes and cash credits, and A., B. and C. should make an excessive importation of foreign goods, say some £5, or £6,000,000, under the English theory and practise they would curtail their circulation £15, or £20,000,000, if necessary, to retain their precious gold-base. Whereas the Scotchman would look upon this course as the height of absurdity and wrong. In such case he would exclaim: "What? shall we, when some gambling stock-jobber, gold-gambler, or a foreign war, shall have created an unusual demand for gold, must we regulate the issues of our banks to reduce the currency as gold is carried off? Rather should we increase our issue, and supply the place of the currency that is exported."

From this property-base the Scotch have built up a cheap, safe, banking and money-system, which is the wonder and admiration of all, wherever it is known. Upon the opposite pretended gold-base, the English government has been enabled to erect and build up a money despotism whose power is felt in every quarter of the globe; yet, never exercised but for the building up of the English aristocracy, and for the extinguishment of liberty and progress among men.

CHAPTER XI.

BANKING IN THE UNITED STATES.

The United States proper as is well known were once colonies of Great Britain, and it was natural that the colonists who came from that country, while protesting against despotism, should from sheer habit adopt the forms of law to which they had been accustomed; although, in these laws were preserved, as in a cabinet, the great essential powers of despotism.

Among these, the commercial and financial laws are its main pillar of support. Banking, therefore, in the United States, is in principle the same as in England. It is based on credit contained in commercial securities, and not on gold or silver. It consists in what is improperly termed, lending money, at the *legal* rate of interest, frequently higher, sometimes lower. The loans are called discounts, because the *rent* or *interest* of the bank-note, is taken out of the customer's note in advance.

The object of banking too, in this country, as in England, "is in making pecuniary gains for the stockholders by legal operations." Treatise on Banking, by A. B. Johnson, Banker, 1850, p. 25.

Several of the colonies issued paper to pay debts. Massachusetts made the first issue of this character in 1690. In 1702, South Carolina made similar issues, and other colonies from time to time, did the same.

But, Pennsylvania made the first and only paper-issue, which can with any propriety be called money. This paper was issued by, and kept entirely under the control of the Provincial Government.

In March 1723, £15,000 was issued. Its loans were to be secured by lands, or by plate deposited in the loan-office. The Act obliged borrowers to pay five per cent. for the sums they took up; made its bills a tender in all payments, on pain of confiscating the debt, or forfeiting the commodity; imposed sufficient penalties on all persons, who presumed to make any bargain or sale on cheaper terms in case of being paid in gold or silver; and provided for the general reduction of the bills, by enacting that one-eighth of the principal, as well as the whole interest should be annually paid. "Governor Pownell, in his work on the Administration of the Colonies, bestows high praise on the paper (money) system of Pennsylvania. "I will venture to say," he declares "that there never was a wiser or better measure, never one better calculated to serve the interests of an increasing country, that there never was a measure more steadily pursued, or more faithfully executed, for forty years together, than the loan-office in Pennsylvania, *founded* and *administered* by the Assembly of that Province." Dr. Franklin, also, bestowed high commendation on the system, and Adam Smith, apparently guided by Governor Pownell and Dr. Franklin, says: "Pennsylvania was always more moderate in its emission of paper-money than any of our other colonies. Its paper currency accordingly *is said* never to have sunk below the value of the gold and silver which was current in the colony before the first emission of its paper-money." Holmes, Vol. II. p. 110—William M. Gouge, History of Banking in the United States, Part II. p. 8.

All things go by comparison. The credit-bills of Pennsylvania were so much better than those of the other Governments, that there was a demand for them throughout the country, for use, in furnishing bills of exchange. It is a mistake, however, that it was never at a discount; gold bore a premium of eleven per cent., and silver at seven, over the currency. But this disproportion between the paper and coin, compared with other colonial currencies was so slight, it does not impair the force of the lesson taught, that under correct laws governmental paper-money has been uniformly good.

The Provincial issues of paper were only evidences of debt, due at a future day issued as the exigencies of the Government might require; a species of governmental script, being neither in form or design money. Though in some cases they were made a legal tender for present use, not as money, but as a debt which the state would at some future time pay. This, with the exception before named, was the real character of the colonial paper, but the people understood it in the light of a debt, they knew the resources of the government, and the authority under which it was issued. If they were injured, it was not by the failure of a bank; but by the government, for which each person was taught to feel that he had some share of the responsibility in its issue, and should therefore take his chances in the losses which might occur by such issue. Like their prototypes in the European world; these colonial governments came far short of making anything like judicious laws for creating this governmental paper, and they utterly failed to make any just provision, either to absorb, by taking it up in taxes, or for its payment.

But as this paper was not in any proper sense of the term money, we do not deem it 'advisable to pursue the history of these paper-issues further than to show, that their true character was in agreement with the ruling ideas of the British public, that nothing was, or could be money, but gold and silver. England had engraved this central idea of her despotism, upon the very brain of the colonists. It is not surprising then, that in all the colonial legislation no change of this fundamental British idea was made, or attempted to be made. The only move looking in that direction, was the attempt to circulate the debt of the colony, as a debt which at some future time should be paid in gold and silver. Thus stood the financial legislation of the colonies up to the time of the Revolution. When the colonies therefore declared their independence, and thereby absolved their allegiance to the British crown, it was natural, that they should continue the same course of legislation. Hence, it will be found that the continental Congress made no change in this particular, and in fact, the legislation and ideas of the commercial and financial classes in this country from that period to the present have been entirely controlled and shaped by this overshadowing influence of the British despotism, made effective through customs, habits and class laws, thence derived. Without further comment, then, we may as well here present an outline of this Revolutionary debt, and the facts as to its subsequent disrepute and non-payment.

The first issue of paper was dated 10th of May, A. D. 1775, but this paper was not actually put into circulation until August following.

The Register of the Treasury, in 1790, estimates that between 1776 and 1781, issues of this class of paper were as follows:

Old issue, $357,476,541; new issue, $2,070,485. The discount, January, 1777, was 1¼ per cent. 1778, 4, and 1779–'7–'8 and '9, 1780, it was 40—and in January 1781, it was 100 per cent. discount, and in May following, it went down to 200, and during the month 500 per cent.

Palatiah Webster, a merchant of Philadelphia, and an uncle of Noah Webster, the grammarian and lexicographer, has given an elaborate account of this continental paper-issue, as viewed from the commercial stand-point, and William M. Gouge, in his history of banking in the United States, has made use of this material to discredit all paper-issues.

Webster is profuse in his denunciation of this continental paper-issue. He says: "If it saved the State, it has also polluted the equity of our laws; turned them into engines of oppression and wrong; corrupted the justice of our public administration; destroyed the fortunes of those who had the most confidence in it; enervated the trade, husbandry and manufactures of our country, and gone far to destroy the morality of our people." It seems, however, not to have occurred to Webster any more than it has, to the commercial and banking class since his day, that the evils described were not simply in the issue of the paper, but in the unjust and class character of the whole money and commercial system—the supreme selfishness which has instituted money upon the principle that it shall answer not only the legitimate purpose of an authentic and just mode of exchange, but that it shall supply the financial and commercial class, at the expense of the industrial classes, commodities and gains, which can only honestly be obtained by labor and at more than triple rates allowed to labor, could not otherwise terminate.

Upon the theory then, that gold and silver constituted the only essential wealth, the continental Congress did not attempt to institute any paper-money system, but issued an evidence of the debt due by the Government; and promised to pay it in gold and silver. As this paper did not pretend to be based upon, or to represent property exchanges, and no provision was made for its payment, it very naturally fell into disrepute. Its decline in value kept pace with the desperate fortunes of war. The dark and gloomy period of 1780 and '81, extinguished whatever of vitality had been infused, or could be galvanized into such a false and dead form by a legislative enactment.

Though this paper-issue has no bearing upon the subject of

governmental-paper-money, or any other paper-money—yet its issue and management, was in principle a just reflex of the British and American paper-money and gold-base systems, and is one out of a thousand instances which have occurred within the last hundred years, where the utter falsity, and downright knavery of the whole system, has been demonstrated again and again. Yet, the men who are the cause of these wrongs, will quote these very wrongs, as an evidence, that state-paper-moneys are not good, and that the system re-vamped in their hands, is the only safe remedy for the injuries they have through it, continued, and will continue to inflict on the people.

That this paper belongs to the bank-robbery gold-base system, and is in no sense a governmental paper-money, will sufficiently appear by the following copy of a Continental Half Dollar.

"No. 182   Half-Dollar.

This bill of Half a Dollar shall entitle the bearer hereof to receive gold or silver, at the rate of four shillings and six-pence sterling, per dollar, for the said bill, according to the resolution of the convention of Maryland, held at Annapolis, 14th day of August, MDCCLXXVI, 1776."

                                                    Signed.

This was printed on a coarse, thick paper, and is in fact a bungling form of a coin obligation clumsily executed. Neither the material upon which it was printed, nor any manner of device was provided for the prevention of counterfeiting, or against over-issues.

The following account from the writings of Thomas Jefferson, by H. A. Washington, Vol. IX., p. 246, demonstrates the correctness of the views here presented, as to the wide-spread prevalence of the British gold theories, as well as the reason why the colonists did not attempt to form a paper-money, and not only so, but it shows in connection with what has been shown, such a condition of public sentiment, derived from the British despotism, that it would have been impossible to have instituted, a just paper-money system.

Mr. Jefferson says, "On the commencement of the late Revolution, Congress had no money. The external commerce of the States being suppressed, the farmer could not sell his produce, and, of course could not pay a tax. Congress had no resources then but in paper-money. Not being able to lay a tax for its redemption, they could only *promise* that taxes should be laid for that purpose so as to redeem the bills by a certain day. They did not foresee the continuance of the war, the almost total suppression of their exports, and other events, which rendered the performance of their engagement impossible."

If then this does not demonstrate that the continental Congress, although they called this national debt issue, " paper-money," never had the idea that it was money, or that it could have been made money, then it would be difficult to find any language strong enough to convey such an idea. That such a class of obligations, thus instituted, should have depreciated, is not at all surprising; the only surprise about it—considering the ideas of Legislators and people concerning money, is, that it should have circulated at all. And especially so, when we further reflect upon the fact that the colonies had from time to time under the influence of these prevailing ideas and previous to the Revolution, issued large quantities of this same class of paper, which had never been paid.

How then this continental coin debt, or in other words, how a promise to pay coin, the country never had, had no means of obtaining, and never made any provision to obtain, has a tendency to show that a good government paper-money cannot be instituted is a question under the facts given, we shall not attempt to argue.

Instead of furnishing any proof against the institution of such a system, it furnishes the very best evidence in its favor. It demonstrates, just what the united history of English banking, for nearly two hundred years teaches, that no corporation or government are, or can be strong enough, and rich enough, to institute a money and a business system, based upon gold or silver, or on a promise to pay in these metals which has been, or can be able, at all times to fulfill such an obligation or promise.

That the life of such a monstrosity, born of despotism, but on free soil in a wild and sparsely populated country, should have been shorter than the struggle for freedom is not strange, and that it should have " died without a groan," and as ignobly as the " wild cat " trash which has succeeded it are continually doing, will very readily be credited.

We have only deemed it necessary to show what the continental money was, as a full answer to all the silly arguments against an " irredeemable paper-money," which has been raised from that source—having as is believed, accomplished that object, the subject of banking in the United States as illustrated by this sketch of colonial history, will be taken up.

The first bank which was instituted in the United States, was the Bank of North America. This bank, at the instance of Robert Morris, Superintendent of Finance under the old Congress, was incorporated by an Act of Congress, on the last day of the year, 1781, and by the Legislature of Pennsylvania, on the first of April, following. It was authorized to hold property, real and personal, to the amount of ten millions of Spanish silver milled dollars and no more. Its capital, therefore, might be just what the stockholders thought proper to make within this limit; and no restrictions whatever were imposed by law on the extent of its issues.

The Bank went into operation, January, 1782, with a *subscribed* capital of $400,000—$254,000 of this sum was taken by Mr. Morris, in behalf of the General Government, and thus giving it entire control. But this capital though *subscribed*, was merely nominal. Governor Morris, speaking of this subscription, says: "I subscribed the sum then remaining in the treasury, being about 254,000 dollars, into the bank stock, per account of the United States, which became thereby the principal stockholder."

William M. Gouge, in his history, in a note to this statement says: "It may be made a question whether the whole of the original capital of the Bank was not advanced by Government." Thomas Paine says, in one of his tracts, "it is well known, that the Bank originated in another Bank, called the Bank of Pennsylvania, which was formed in the spring of 1780. On the 17th of June, it was resolved to open a security subscription to the amount of 300,000 pounds, Pennsylvania currency, in real money, the subscribers to *execute bonds* for the amount of their subscription, and to form a Bank for supplying the army." He afterwards speaks of these subscriptions being transferred to the Bank of North America.

"From the Journals of Congress, it appears that the Board of Treasury was directed to deposit in this Pennsylvania Bond-Bank," bills of exchange, in favor of the directors thereof, on the Ministers of the United States in Europe, or any of them, and in such sums as shall be thought convenient, but not to exceed in the whole £150,000 sterling.

The Bank probably had $70,000 with which to commence its

proper operations. On this amount, says Gouge, "it undertook to make advances to the Government and to individuals ; but as the experience of evils of *continental money* was fresh in the minds of the people, some difficulty was encountered in giving currency to the notes of the Bank. To remove this *prejudice*, the gentlemen who were interested in the institution, were, as we have learned from undoubted authority, in the practice of requesting people from the country and laboring men about town to go to the Bank and get silver in exchange. When, on this errand of a neighborly kindness, as they thought it, they found a display of silver on the counter, and men employed in raising boxes containing silver, or supposed to contain silver, from the cellar into the banking room, or lowering them from the banking-room into the cellar. By contrivances like these, the Bank obtained the reputation of possessing immense wealth, but its hollowness was several times nearly made apparent; especially on one occasion, when one of the co-partners withdrew a deposit of some five, or six thousand dollars, when the whole specie stock of the Bank did not probably exceed twenty thousand dollars."

By these means, and the funds of the General Government, the bank-notes became current. Its early dividends were from 12 to 16 per cent. The stockholders were moderately well satisfied with this annual income as they had furnished none of the capital, they thought it would answer, but felt a strong desire not to extend an opportunity to others to reap such small legislative advantages. This started the project for a new bank, to defeat this, an increase of stock was offered, but not without a long and loud protest against the hardship of being obliged to receive new partners.

During the year 1784, the Bank issued paper freely, and in 1785, a great, and the usual bank-scarcity of money followed. Upon petitions from citizens of Chester and Bucks counties, setting forth the character of these grievances, the Legislature on 13th September, 1785, repealed the law granting the charter. This Repealing Act, very possibly may have been the origin, or at least have given shape to the constitutional provision upon that class of subjects.

The Bank, however, continued its business under the Act of Congress. A contest was soon renewed in the Pennsylvania Legislature for a re-charter, which was at first refused, but public virtue is not bomb-proof against bank assaults, and in 1787, the Bank with limited powers was re-chartered and has been continued down to the present time.

Thus banking was instituted in the United States, without any of the pretended capital, which is described in bank charters, except on paper, and it has been continued from that day to the present, without any limitation or restriction other than such as the bank interest requires. As this pretended capital which the bank had, was only the money which passed through it, belonging to the United States, it will be readily perceived that bank-interest and bank-dividends are not the rent or interest paid to the bank for their capital, but a license granted to them by law, whereby the public are compelled to pay so much tariff to this special class for permitting the evidences of value to be a monopoly in their hands, and the amount of tariff thus imposed, above the cost of transacting all the business at high rates, besides official stealings, are exhibited in the annual dividends. An annual dividend therefore, of from 12 to 16 per cent., is under the circumstances very good evidence that banking is instituted "to make money" without an idea of rendering any return for such extraordinary privileges.

We have thus traced the outlines of the banking and money theory, through the Colonial and Revolutionary periods of our history far enough to show, how deeply England had imbedded her peculiarly grasping and overreaching system, into the minds not only of the legislative and financial classes, but that all classes, were more or less affected with her prevailing gold and silver-money theories. It has also been shown, that, the moment the Revolutionary period closed, Robert Morris, who had been the Financial Superintendent of the continental government, prepared and obtained an Act for a Bank, without any limit to its paper-issues—that this Bank without capital, by the aid of the government's money, and the divers frauds copied from its English prototype, was enabled to wring out of labor as a surplus profit above all expenses from 12 to 16 per cent. dividends. This was the promising origin and model design of American banking. A system which has abstracted from American labor a larger sum than slavery and war both combined. We are now to trace its connection, and its bearing more particularly upon govern- and people, under our present National and State constitutions and governments.

An Act to incorporate the first Bank of the United States, under the Constitution, passed the Senate, on the 20th January, 1791, and the House on the 8th February following, and on the 14th of the same month, it was signed by the President. This Act was *par excellence* the model of American banking. A more careful synopsis therefore, of some of its provisions will be given, than would otherwise be deemed necessary.

The nominal capital of this bank was ten millions of dollars, one-fifth part of which was subscribed by the National Government; but the Government having no money to pay, proposed to borrow it from the Bank—and the Bank having no money to lend, passed a *credit* of two millions on its books to the Government on which it paid six per cent. The Government, in its turn, received the dividends on 500 shares of stock, of 400 dollars each at par value.

The residue of the capital, eight millions, subscribed by individuals was to be paid, three-fourths in six per cent.-stock, and one-fourth in specie, in four six-monthly instalments of five hundred thousand dollars each. "No more," says Dr. Erich Bollman, " or little more than the first installment, can ever be considered as having been received by the Bank actually in hard money. "The capital of the United States Bank, under the Charter of April 10th, 1816, its first renewal, was thirty-five millions. The Government subscribed seven millions, having no money the Bank granted it a credit. The twenty-eight millions of stock were subscribed for by individuals—on each share they were to pay five dollars in gold or silver coin at the time of subscribing; in six months, ten dollars, at twelve, ten dollars. " At each of those three periods twenty-four dollars more were to be paid on each share, either in United States stock, or in gold and silver coin, at the option of the subscribers."

No more, or very little more than the first instalment of five dollars on each share was paid in coin. The Directors decided, that no more was necessary. "It is clear," says one of them, " that the Bank having commenced business, and put its paper in circulation, it could not enforce the specie part of the second and third instalments in new acquisitions of specie. The Directors acted wisely in discounting the notes of the stockholders, payable in specie, sixty days after date for the payment of the second instalment."

It is claimed by cyclopediasts, statistical, financial and other classes of public writers in the bank-interest, that the Congress of the United States having experienced great difficulties in providing requisite means for carrying on the war, were induced to establish "The Bank of North America," and that this rendered great aid to the Government, in closing the war.

But William M. Gouge has shown that the capture of Cornwallis took place on the 9th of October, 1781, which, unless historians are greatly at fault, strongly presaged an early close of the war, besides, the Bank did not go into operation until January 7th, 1782.

1. The whole expenditures in 1782, was only $3,600,000, and in 1783, $3,000,000, and these amounts were raised by loans in Europe, and by increased taxation.

2. The testimony of Robert and Governor Morris, shows that the amount subscribed by individuals to the Bank did not exceed $70,000.

3. Robert Morris, in the Pennsylvania Legislature, did not claim that the excess of silver-money advanced by the Bank, ever exceeded the Government deposits, $165,000, and generally not $50,000.

So that the aid rendered was not very essential. But a careful survey of the facts leads to this conclusion, that the bank or money-sharks followed the Government. Their exceeding patriotism did not lead them to invest so permanently in continental money, as in preying upon the Government, making use of the misfortunes of the country to gather out of it the material to institute a National Bank, and afterwards the establishment of the State Jayhawking system, which up to our late Revolution has borne unlimited sway—accordingly it will be found: "First, that this Bank Charter provided, that its subscribed capital of $10,000,000, shall be payable, one-fourth in gold and silver, and three-fourths in that part of the public *debt*, which according to the loan proposed, in the fourth and fifteenth sections of the Act, entitled an Act, making provision for the debt of the United States, shall bear an accruing interest, at the time of payment, of six per centum per annum, and shall also be payable in four equal parts, in the aforesaid ratio of specie to debt, at the distance of six calendar months from each other; the first shall be paid at the time of subscription."

Second, that no bank should be established by any future law of the United States, during the continuance of the corporation thereby created, and for which the faith of the United States was pledged.

The Act was drawn by Alexander Hamilton, the great admirer and copyist of English despotism. Every advantageous clause of the English Act was copied, and such additions were made to it, as would be likely to be useful to the bank-owners, or could be rendered available in gathering into their hands the fruits of the annual industries.

We thus see how the American banking-system was inaugurated. It was born of the misfortune and miseries of war. But why was the continental *paper-money* permitted to die. We venture to suggest for the benefit of the banking advocates, that there were stronger reasons for its sudden exit, than its being a state-paper-money. It had then answered all the purposes of the Revolution, which it could be made to answer. It had gone into the hands of the industrial and business classes, who were possessed of an unusual share of patriotism. It could not be resurrected as a currency for the benefit of the banking-class, any more than a dead " wild cat bank," and it furnished no six per cent. base for " wild cat " banking.

There was therefore very good reason why it should have died—it accordingly did die—but there are diverse other good reasons which could be given, that should prevent " wild cat " bankers from exhuming its defunct carcass, or from exhibiting its bloody bones either as a warning against instituting state-paper monies, or as an admonition in favor of their wicked system, built upon its ruins. If the Continental was worthless, it did not further defraud or trouble the people, with baseless promises, but the new did, and still continues to do.

But to return to the bank history—it was incorporated under the name and style of " The President, Directors, and Company of the Bank of the United States," and to continue until March 4th, 1811. It was located at Philadelphia with branches at different points. It made dividends from 8 to 10 per cent. per annum, much lower than had been made by the Bank of North America, the decline of profits being attributable to the creation of new banks. An application for the renewal of the charter was made in 1808, three years before it would expire, but this application was pressed by Mr. Gallatin, and remained before Congress until February 5th, 1811, when a bill was brought forward, and on the 20th was defeated. The Bank was obliged to wind up its affairs, and it eventually paid its stockholders 108½ per cent. on its stock.

In the war of 1812–'15, the Government was engaged in war, and under great financial embarrassment by the bank-suspensions which were then existing. In this condition of financial affairs, Alexander J. Dallas was called to the head of the Treasury, and under his manipulation, Congress in about a fortnight were duly prepared to usher in a new United States Bank. On the 20th January, 1815, a bill was passed by Congress, but President Madison vetoed it, and on the 3d of April, a bill, which had previously passed the House of Representatives, was adopted by the Senate, received the signature of the President, and became a law. The title of this institution was "The President, Directors, and Company of the Bank of the United States." Its capital was to be $35,000,000, composed 350,000 shares, $100 each, $7,000,000 of the stock was to be subscribed by the United States, and the remaining $28,000,000, by individuals, companies, or corporations. The charter was to continue in force until March 3, 1836, and to commence business so soon as $8,400,000, exclusive of the government subscription, was paid in. It was prohibited lending to the United States more than $500,000, or to any State more than $50,000, or to any foreign prince any sum whatever without the sanction of a law previously obtained.

This Bank went into operation January 7th, 1817, with no more than about one per cent. of its capital paid in, but through its agency the other banks resumed specie- payments, and business went on swimmingly under a " specie-basis"

This resumption of specie-payments was secured by an agreement between the United States Bank and the State Banks, that the resumption of specie-payments should take place on the 20th of February on condition, among others, that the Bank of the United States should not demand payment of any balances of the State institutions, until that bank and its branches should have discounted for individuals not having duties to pay, at some of the principal Atlantic ports, to the amount of $6,000,000.

It will thus be seen that this clamor about specie payments, is a question not as to the goodness of a currency, but a question of interest to bankers and importers, in which under the banking and gold laws, as will be seen in the sequel, the rights of the people are sacrificed at most enormous rates.

As soon as this arrangement between the banks had been effected every effort was put forth on the part of the officers of the United States Bank to push its paper into circulation. In the course of little more than a month, its discounts had been extended from three to twenty millions of dollars, and by the end of October of the same year, thirty-three millions. Its issues seem only to have been limited by the inability of the President and Cashier to sign notes.

These extraordinary issues, or discounts were, to a considerable extent, made to stockholders on a pledge of their stock at par, without other securities, with a view to aid them in paying up the balance of their stock. Schemers and gambling stock-jobbers were thereby enabled without property or capital, to become large owners and dealers in the capital stock. Not one-third of the $7,000,000 of coin which the charter required, was ever paid. High prices and wild speculation everywhere prevailed. In eighteen months this gold-base and specie paying regulator, was obliged rapidly to contract its issues. A severe money-panic was on hand, the business of the country prostrated, and its losses might be counted by millions. The President of the Bank, Mr. Cheves, reported the losses of the Bank to be considerably over $3,500,000, previous to March 6th, 1819, and besides, dividends had been made to the amount of $4,410,000.

This furnishes a specimen of "specie" payments, and what is meant by "strengthening the public credit" by gold-base, and coin paying laws, viz.: an open, bare-faced robbery of the people under color of these laws. An instance cannot be found, where these financial disasters and direct robbery of the people, may not be traced to these extremely partial and unjust financial laws as the cause. Arising out of this gross bank-mismanagement in 1818, an ineffectual attempt was made to repeal the charter, but it failed. In 1829, President Jackson, in his annual message, intimated that constitutional difficulties might prevent a re-charter, and desired the early consideration of this matter by Congress. On the 4th of July, 1832, a bill to re-charter the Bank passed by Congress, was sent to the President, who on the 10th returned it with his veto. A violent attempt was made to pass it over the veto, but it failed, and on March 3d, 1836, by the limitation of the charter the Bank expired. It was re-chartered as a state institution, the same year, by the Legislature of Pennsylvania, with the same amount of capital. In 1837, it suspended specie-payments, but finally suspended February 6th. It had sunk its whole capital and nothing remained for the stock-holders.

While the fight against the United States Bank was purely political yet, there is no question, but that there was a larger opposition to the Bank which sprang out of the rivalry of the State Bank power, which was then beginning to loom up to view. There were previous to the establishment of what is called the "National Banking" system, some 1,600 of these State institutions. In the six New England States there were in 1856, 257; in New York, 507 banks and branches, with a pretended capital of $114,611,752. .The first Bank which went regularly into operation in any of the States was established in the city of Boston, in 1784, where it still exists.

These banks are generally created by special charter, though "free banking" laws exist in Vermont, Massachusetts and Connecticut. The "Suffolk bank system," heretofore, has played an important part in the New England banking system.

The system originated with five banks in Boston, each appointing each one member of a committee, to superintend and manage the operations of collecting the notes of foreign banks. An agent of this committee received, credited and kept an account of all the foreign money taken by these banks. The expenses of collecting, keeping an account, as well as the losses on the foreign money were to be borne by these institutions, in proportion to the amount received on deposit by each. The entire management of these operations was eventually placed under the control of the Suffolk Bank. Each Bank made a stipulated deposit, in the aggregate amounting to $300,000, on which no interest was paid. As by degrees, the country banks made their deposits, those of the other banks were from time to time reduced. The Suffolk Bank redeemed the bills of all the New England Banks depositing with it at par. Through this agency a working capital of $1,000,000 is furnished at the mere cost of the salaries of the clerks. The annual amount of redemption made is about $350,000,000. With a view of taking part of this business, The Bank of Mutual Redemption was chartered in 1855. The first bank in New York, was the Manhattan, established in 1799. The number of banks operating in the State of New York, in 1855, was 311, capital, $96,381,301. In 1829, the Legislature of New York, vainly hoping it could alleviate some of the evils of this false plundering system, instituted what was called "The safety fund-system," by which each bank was required to contribute annually to a joint fund, equal to one-half of one per cent. upon its capital deposited with the Treasurer of the State, as a bank-fund, until it should amount to three per cent. on the capital of the banks. This fund to be applied in the redemption of the bills of such as should fail. The failure of ten banks amounting to about $2,500,000, considerably more than swallowed up the funds, and the system was abandoned. In 1838, a "free banking law" was passed, permitting any individual, or association to engage in banking, by depositing with the State comptroller the stocks of the United States, or of any State, which were equal to five per cent. stocks; and bonds and mortgages on real estate worth twice the amount of the mortgages over and above all buildings thereon, and leaving interest at the rate of six per cent., per annum. On receipt of such securities, the parties furnishing the same were to receive an equal amount of notes numbered, registered and signed. But here again the chronic difficulties of banking invaded this system. It was found, these securities were not "convertible," and in 1840, two years after the passage of the Act, the law was so amended as to require stocks of either the United States or of New York, or bonds and mortgages were required as security. Weekly returns of the condition of the banks, in the City of New York, are required to be published, and in 1853, a clearing house was established in that city.

General banking laws, or "free-banking," has been instituted in New Jersey, Virginia, Indiana, Illinois, Wisconsin, Tennessee, Louisiana and Pennsylvania, they have so far simply proved stupenduous swindles. They were pretty effectually wiped out by the late rebellion, in the new States, to be replaced by a new breed of "Wild Cats," under national authority popularly denominated "National Banking." The whole number of State banks, in 1860, amounted to 1,600.

The following will illustrate the manner in which the "convertible" and reliable gold-base mixed currency is put into circulation, and the people soundly protected against the evils of an "irredeemable" State-currency: A committee appointed by the Legislature of Rhode Island, to examine into the irregularities committed by the official Board of "The Farmer's Exchange Bank of Gloucester," among other things report: That the Bank was incorporated in 1804. The capital stock was $100,000, divided into two thousand shares, fifty dollars each, payable in seven instalments, in gold or silver. Some stock-holders paid their shares, others part, and gave their notes for the residue. The Directors lodged the amount of their first instalment, but received the amount a few days afterwards in bills on their individual notes without security. They then gave five notes without indorsers, for the five first instalments payable on demand with interest; for the two last no payment was made or security given. The said notes remained in the Bank until the Directors transferred their stock, when they were delivered up, in the manner hereinafter mentioned.

The Directors were the holders of one hundred and three shares each, and in this manner did the Farmer's Exchange Bank, which by the charter was to consist of two thousand shares, commence its operations with only six hundred and sixty-one shares, on which any payments had been made in gold and silver, agreeably to the express provisions of the charter; and the whole money paid into the Bank at any one period whatever, on the said six hundred and sixty-one shares, amounted to nineteen thousand one hundred and forty-one dollars and eighty-six cents.

"Prior to the 29th of March, 1808, sundry stock-holders, holding four hundred and fifty shares, transferred them to the Directors of said Bank. No money, or other consideration whatever, was paid by the Directors with their own property to any of the stock-holders who so transferred their shares, but they were uniformly paid for with the property of the corporation. Most of the said stock-holders were indebted to the Bank in notes, and to them their notes were given up, and if their shares exceeded the sum due from them to the Bank, the balance was paid out of the Bank with the property of the said corporation; and none of the said Directors, or any person whatever, was debited for the said sums so paid, or for the notes surrendered."

On the third day of June, 1805, the Board of Directors passed a vote permitting each Director to take out of the Bank 200 dollars for the purpose of exchanging the same. The said Directors have never paid or accounted for said money to the Bank.

When the Bank first commenced its operations, the capital paid in including the money paid by the Directors, and which was soon after repaid to them, as herein before stated, amounted 'to the sum of eleven thousand eight hundred and six dollars and sixty-one cents; when the Directors had as before stated, taken back in bills the amount they had paid in specie for their first instalment. The capital stock really paid in, amounted to only the sum of three thousand and eighty-one dollars and eleven cents."

"The Directors never declared any certain dividend of the profits of the Bank, but once a year paid to the stock-holders interest, generally at the rate of eight per cent. per annum, on the sums they had respectively paid in, and the residue amounting in some years to one hundred and thirty dollars each, the Directors divided among themselves.

"According to the books containing the weekly state of the Bank, there were several periods when the amount of bills in circulation far exceeded the amount of notes due the Bank; for instance, on the twenty-fifth day of March, 1805, the amount of bills in circulation was seventy-two thousand two hundred and eleven dollars, and the amount of debts due the Bank, was fifty-three thousand two hundred and seventy-five dollars; at some periods, anterior to the 29th day of March, 1808, the Bank had in circulation from sixty to seventy thousand dollars. On the 28th day of March, 1808, there was in said Bank, in specie and bills of other Banks, three hundred and eighty dollars and fifty cents, and the Bank had twenty-two thousand five hundred and twenty-four dollars of their own bills in circulation."

"Under this system, the Bank continued in operation about four years; and then eleven of the Directors transferred their interest in the institution to the agent of Andrew Dexter, Jr., of Boston. Each of the Directors received thirteen hundred dollars, on consideration of his transferring his shares; and each of them received back the notes he had given for instalments, the whole principal and interest whereof were then due to the Bank. The thirteen hundred dollars were paid to some of the Directors by notes signed by Simon Smith, and John Harris, as principals, and Andrew Dexter, Jr., as surety; to others by surrendering them notes given by the Bank for money borrowed, and to others by giving them the notes of individuals which were the property of the Bank. It appears that all the money paid to the Directors, was paid out of the Bank with the property of the corporation, except that there is charged to said Dexter, three thousand seven hundred and eighty-five dollars and ninety-five cents paid on that account." Dexter thus got control of the institution, and having a Board of Directors disposed to favor his views, he got from the Bank, at divers times in the course of the year, its bills to the amount of seven hundred and sixty thousand two hundred and sixty-five dollars, and there was paid to sundry persons for his use, three thousand seven hundred and eighty-five dollars and ninety-five cents."

"From the first connection of Dexter with the Bank, he appears, by himself and his agents, to have had the entire control and management thereof; all his schemes and plans, however wild and extravagant, were adopted and carried into execution without reserve ; those of the Directors who still pretended to superintend the concerns of the Bank, took no care whatever to guard the interest of the stock-holders or the public."

Dexter was furnished with as much money as he thought proper to demand, and prescribed his own terms as to the security he gave, the rate of interest, and the time and manner of payment, the greatest secrecy was used respecting his negociations at the Bank to prevent the public from being alarmed at the immense sum of money which was so suddenly put in circulation; and at the request of Dexter, the cashier signed the bills secretly and chiefly in the night. Dexter never gave any security whatever, except his own name, for any money received by him from the Bank. For the first sums delivered, Dexter gave his receipts, for other sums he gave receipts to the follow-ing purport: that he would employ the money as their agent for their benefit, paying them six per cent. interest therefor, and redeeming the bills by paying specie as often as they returned to the Bank; after these receipts had been standing for some time, they were taken up by Dexter, and a note given by him for the whole amount of the tenor and effect following: " I, Andrew Dexter, Jr., do promise the President, Directors and Company of the Farmer's Exchange Bank, to pay them on order ———— dollars, in two years from the date, with interest, at two per cent. per annum ; it being however understood that said Dexter shall not be called upon to make payment, until he thinks proper, he being the principal stockholder, and best knowing when it will be proper to pay the same." The said note was afterwards given to Dexter, and a note given by him for five hundred and seven thousand seven hundred and seventy-one dollars, bearing date on the 30th of November, 1808; all the money received by Dexter after that time was delivered to him by order of Harris and Fairbanks, the last of which was delivered on the ninth of February, 1809, for which Dexter gave his notes, which are now remaining in the Bank; one bearing date on the 4th of November, 1808, for three hundred thousand dollars, one bearing date on the 30th of the same month for thirty-two thousand dollars, and one bearing date on the 12th day of December, 1808, for six thousand dollars ; all which notes amount to the sum of eight hundred and fifty-five thousand, seven hundred and seventy-one dollars, payable in eight years from their respective dates, bearing interest at and after the rate of two per cent. per annum.

"Out of the amount above stated, as due from the said Andrew Dexter, Jr., to the Bank, ought to be deducted certain drafts or orders drawn, on said Dexter, by the Cashier, to take up the bills, at different times returned to the Bank, so far as the said drafts or orders have been paid by said Dexter, the amount of said drafts or orders, according to the books of the bank, still outstanding and unsettled, is two hundred and four thousand and five dollars, but of this sum the committee have no means of ascertaining what part has been paid by the said Dexter.

"In December, 1808, the credit of the Bank had become very low, and the bills were selling at a large discount, but the said Andrew Dexter, Jr., and the other persons who managed the affairs of the Bank, instead of putting a stop to the emission of their bills, and making some provision for the payment of those in circulation, redoubled their efforts to circulate sums to a large amount, when at the same time they refused the payment of the smallest sums at the Bank.

"The President and the cashier were incessantly employed in signing bills, and Dexter was continually urging them to sign bills as fast as possible, telling them that everything depended on his having them very speedily; that if they were not soon finished, he should not be able to dispose of them, and at that time he should be able to sell some of them very well. The bills were made with so much precipitation, and the officers of the Bank were so much pressed for time, that said bills were in some instances sent to Boston without being dated or numbered.

"There is now in said Bank, eighty-six dollars and forty-six cents of specie. On the 9th of February, 1809 there had been emitted by said bank six hundred and forty-eight thousand and forty-three dollars of their bills, according to their books, owing to the extreme confusion in which their mode of keeping their accounts has involved all their transactions, it is impossible to ascertain with precision the amount of their bills now in circulation; but from the enquiries and examinations made by the committee, they are of the opinion that other bills of said bank now in circulation, amount to the enormous sum of five hundred eighty thousand dollars."

From the testimony of the cashier, which is appended to the report, it appears that the emission of six hundred and forty-eight thousand eight hundred and forty-three dollars bank-bills, spoken of by the Committee, took place between the 29th of March, 1808, and the 9th of February, 1809, and that previous to the first mentioned date, the bank had bills in circulation to the amount of forty-five thousand eight hundred and twenty-one dollars.

The history of the Farmer's Bank of Gloucester, shows what cunning men can do, when they have a legislative charter to work with. When the explosion took place, other New England Banks exhibited proof that they had been trading on the same principles, though none we believe to the same extent.

Another specimen of a mixed currency, based upon specie, will be found in the case of " The Sutton Bank, incorporated March 11th, 1828. The Act provided that the capital-stock of said corporation shall consist of one hundred dollars in gold and silver, to be divided into shares of one hundred dollars each, which shall be paid in the manner following, viz. : one-half part on or before the first day of October (then) next, and the remaining part thereof, on or before the first day of March, in the year of our Lord, one thousand eight hundred and twenty-nine. It further provided, " that no moneys shall be loaned or discounts made, nor shall any bills or promissory notes be made or issued from the said Bank, until the capital actually paid in, and existing in gold and silver in said vaults, shall amount to fifty thousand dollars, nor until the capital-stock, actually in said vaults shall have been inspected and examined by three Commissioners, to be appointed by the Governor for that purpose, whose duty it shall be, at the expense of the said corporation to examine the money actually existing in said vaults, and to ascertain by oaths of the Directors of said Bank, or a majority of them, that the said capital-stock hath been *bona fide* paid in by the stock-holders of said Bank, and towards the payment of their respective shares, and not intended for any other purpose, and that it is intended there to remain as part of said capital."

On the 26th day of September, 1828, the Governor in compliance with an application for that purpose, made by a committee of the subscribers for stock in said Sutton Bank, appointed commissioners to examine the moneys actually existing in vaults of said bank as is provided in the second section of their Act of incorporation. On the 27th of September, 1828, the Sutton Bank borrowed, on a deposit of fifty-one thousand dollars in the bills of the City Bank the sum of fifty thousand dollars in specie for one day only; this same specie was examined by the Commissioners, and the following certificates made out, viz.:

"We, the subscribers, Commissioners appointed for that purpose, have this day been shown, and have examined fifty thousand dollars in specie, in the vaults of the Sutton Bank, which was paid in by the stockholders as their first instalment, agreeably to their Act of Incorporation, passed the eleventh day of March, 1828.

September 27th, 1828.

JONATHAN LELAND,
AMASA ROBERTS, } *Commissioners.*
SAMUEL WOOD,

"Suffolk, ss. Boston, Sept. 27th, 1828.

Then personally appeared Hezekiah Howe, Jonas L. Sibley, Joshua W. Leland and Thomas Harback, being a majority of Directors of Sutton Bank, and made oath that fifty thousand dollars in specie by them shown in their vaults, was the first instalment paid by the stock-holders of the Bank towards the payment of their respective shares, and not for any other purpose, and that it is intended therein to remain a part of said capital. Before me,

ELIPHALET WILLIAMS, *Just. Peace.*"

"The bills and specie were then re-exchanged; the whole business accomplished in an hour, and all of it done within the walls of the City Bank, in the City of Boston."

We might continue to give instances of a similar character, until a volume three times the size of the present one, would be filled, and still not begin to exhibit a tithe of this fraudulent system. Indeed the only way this subject could be exhausted would be by giving the history of every bank instituted since the organization of the Government down to the present moment. Out of the whole list not an instance can be found where a bank has been instituted upon a *bona fide* cash-capital. The instances here given of the mode of forming banks upon a specie-basis, are much more than a fair ordinary average of the whole system. We do not deem it necessary, either to continue this branch of the subject further, or to give a more specific unfolding of the manner in which the *currency* circulation of the country is sustained, without anything more than the nominal capital we have here shown to be its base, until we have unfolded the present so called "National Banking" system. The former system was merely a sham and a fraud—this is an organized system of National robbery, copied from the English, and the most stupendous swindle the world has ever beheld. The English system as will be seen, is a mere huckster establishment beside it—their banking based on bonds, is £14,000,000, or about $70,000,000, ours $300,000,000, and our interest is about double that of England.

The following are some of the leading provisions of the so called "National Banking" Act:

Sec. 1 provides, That the chief officer of the Bureau of Currency shall be styled "*the Comptroller of the Currency*," and shall be under the general direction of the Secretary of the Treasury. He shall be appointed by the President, upon the nomination of the Secretary of the Treasury with the advice and consent of the Senate. Term of office, five years, unless sooner removed by the President with consent of the Senate; salary, five thousand dollars per annum. To have a deputy, who shall be appointed by the Secretary of the Treasury, with a salary of two thousand five hundred dollars; the Comptroller is empowered to employ the necessary clerks to discharge such duties, as he shall direct, which clerks shall be appointed and classified by the Secretary of the Treasury. The Comptroller and deputy shall take the oath of office prescribed by the constitution and laws of the United States and give bonds, the former, one hundred thousand dollars, and the latter fifty thousand dollars, with security approved by the Secretary of the Treasury.

Sec. 11 and 46 Confers on every association organized under this act, general banking powers, and authorizes the taking or receiving of such rates of interest as may be fixed by the laws of the States and Territories in which such banking association may be located, and provides that such rates of interest may be taken in advance.

SEC. 16 and 41 provides, That every bank, organized under this act, upon depositing with the Secretary of the Treasury United States six per cent., interest bonds, shall receive from the Comptroller circulating notes equal in amount to ninety per cent. of the current market value of the bonds deposited, but not to exceed the par value thereof; and that every association shall keep on hand, in lawful money of the United States, twenty-five per cent. of its outstanding notes of circulation for the redemption thereof: *Provided*, That clearing house certificates and balances due from other associations, in good standing, and subject to sight draft, may be counted as part of such reserve to the amount of three-fifths thereof.

SEC. 17 provides, That the entire circulation shall not exceed three hundred millions of dollars, one-half of which is to be apportioned to the several States and Territories, according to their representative population, and the remainder is to be apportioned by the Secretary of the Treasury among the States and Territories, paying due regard to the existing banking capital, resources and business of such States and Territories.

SEC. 26, 27 and 28 provides, That when any bank shall fail or refuse to redeem its circulating notes with lawful money, (legal tender, Treasury notes,) the Comptroller may declare the stocks pledged forfeited to the United States, or so much thereof as may be necessary to redeem its circulation, and pay its circulating notes out of the United States Treasury; or he may sell such stocks at public auction, in the city of New York; or he may, if in his opinion the interest of the United States would be promoted thereby, sell such stocks at private sale, and receive therefor either money or the notes of such failing association: *Provided*, no such bonds shall be sold at private sale for less than their par value, nor for less than their current market value at the time of sale.

SEC. 18 and 19 provides, That the Comptroller, under the direction of the Secretary of the Treasury, shall procure the dies and plates for printing the notes for circulation, and print and deliver the notes to the banking association, and all expenses incurred thereby shall be audited and paid as contingent expenses of the treasury department. And for the purpose reimbursing the same, and all other expenses incurred under this act, and in lieu of all taxes upon the circulation authorized by this act, or upon the bonds deposited for the security of the same, the associations organized under this act, shall pay annually to the Comptroller, in lawful money, (Treasury notes,) one-half of one per cent. on the amount of circulating notes received by such association.

Sec. 54, Authorizes the Secretary of the Treasury to employ any of such associations as depositories of the public money, except the receipts from customs.

Sec. 65., Reserves to Congress the right, at any time, to amend, alter or repeal this act.

This presents enough of the Act to show that in principle there is no essential difference between the State "Wild Cat" system and the National. The National, however, does not pretend to base the issue of paper upon the gilded device of a *gold-base*, but it substitutes by solemn injunction on the banker, that he shall keep on hand "in lawful money of the United States, twenty-five per cent. of *its outstanding notes* of circulation for the redemption thereof: *Provided*, That clearing house certificates and balances due from other associations in *good standing* and subject to sight draft, may be counted as part of such reserve to the amount of three-fifths thereof. In other words, the bankers are required to hold in their breeches pockets, or vaults, certificates which they have exchanged with each other, to the amount of fifteen per cent., and ten dollars of legal tenders of their own, or their depositors, with which to redeem a hundred dollars of their own notes. If, however, the bankers under the stronger provision of State laws, and under the solemnities of an oath, could not be relied upon to hold securities of silver and gold, certainly they cannot reasonably be expected to find pockets or vaults strong enough to hold "legal tenders," or banker's certificates any better; but, even if they could, the fund is entirely inadequate for the purposes of redemption. But the truth is, that under neither system is any attention paid to such provisions further than to be on a lookout not to forfeit their special privileges; the fund relied upon for redemption is the avails of the customers' notes, and the surplus deposits generally on hand; gold and silver, legal tenders, and bank-certificates in "good standing," cut no figure in the matter of redemption—they are merely the clap-trap, or 'stool-pigeon for the amusement of the public. Under this system it is important to make a big exhibit of pretended securities otherwise the naked deformity and downright robbery of the system would be too bare-faced and outrageous to be tolerated. Stripped stark naked, the people would soon discover that royalty, or the bankers special class privileges, even in a republican or democratic garb, differs from robbery only in the silk gauze covering of law. There is no essential difference between banking under State laws, and that of the so called National banking system. Neither systems are intended to establish justice in the national finance, both are intended to make unjust gain under color of law, and therefore the issues of paper, under neither, are based upon the capital of the banker, but practically upon that of the people. Lest this point should be overlooked by not having been made sufficiently clear, we will proceed to illustrate it by bank returns, March, 1836, Bank of United States circulation, $19,195'817; specie, $12,175,476; deposits, $16,759,667. How could this bank pay $16,759,667, with $12,175,476, and redeem its notes with specie. The Commissioner's Reports of the banks of Connecticut, from 1837 to 1849, twelve years, shows an average circulation of $11,669,457, and an average of $478,719 of specie, four per cent. on every one hundred dollars of paper. And it is more than probable that a majority of this specie, if not the whole, belonged to depositors and not to the bank owners.

This exhibit of capital is not materially improved under the National Banking Act, this does not require either coin or bullion for the redemption of the notes. The requirement that bankers shall keep on hand fifteen per cent. of banker's certificates and ten per cent. "legal tenders," may produce any amount of bank frauds and perjury, but if this is the fund relied upon for redemption, as has been shown it is not adequate for that purpose. The pledge of bonds with the Secretary for the ultimate redemption of the notes, has no bearing upon this question. Such security really gives no present efficiency or value to the paper as money, for the reason, that business demands in making an exchange, a legalized tally or counter of the commodity, which is a legal equivalent for every commodity at its market value. A bond, or note therefore, bearing six per cent. interest, payable semi-annually, and the principal at twenty years, does not fill this money requirement. Hence then, neither national bonds, legal tenders, nor banker's certificates, are what give efficiency and value, to banker's notes as money, but it is the notes and securities given by the business public. The value of these depend upon the value and use made of the property purchased from the industrial classes.

The annual productions of the United States may be estimated at something over $1,500,000,000.

If we suppose profits and interest amount to forty per cent., then the security for the banker's notes may be thus expressed:

Farmer's property................$1,500,000,000
Profits on first sales..............   600,000,000
                                     ─────────────
                                      $2,100,000,000

This $2,100,000,000, will be good collateral security, and a reliable fund with which to redeem $1,500,000,000 banker's notes, and the interest. No other capital is required or used. Those indebted to the bank will be glad to get this $1,500,000,000 of bank-notes, to take up their $2,100,000,000 of individual notes. Estimating the farmer's products in second hands at $2,100,000,000—this would give the farmers $1,500,000,000, and the banking and business class $600,000,000, or estimated at first cost, it makes a distribution of the farmer's property as follows:

Farmers........................$1,071,428,620
Bankers and business class........   428,571,380

The farmers have sold their $1,500,000,000 of produce at market price, and got $1,071,428,620, and they cannot tell precisely how this metamorphose of values was effected, or how in the end a majority of their surplus productions got out of their hands, and into the hands of those who do not labor, or perform much useful service.

If however, there is a desire to find out this injustice, it can be directly traced to these unjust bond and banking laws. They make a gross monopoly of money and of business. The business class perform an actual service in making exchanges. The banking class produce nothing, control the exchanges by a monopoly created by law, perform a very trifling service, and reap large gains, mere class laws perquisites. They furnish no actual capital. Their office is principally that of bookkeepers of the nation's industries, being by law allowed a pension, rent, or *interest* out of these industries four times the value of the service rendered.

Banker's notes are used in the place of account books, and redemption of their notes is a simple cancellation or balancing of accounts through the machinery of bank-bills, promissory notes, and other commercial obligations, or securities. For this book-keeping service, by a series of class laws, the bankers have secured to themselves without useful service about one-seventh of the productions of the nation as an annual tribute due to these modern " Cesars "—or in other words their annual income, or seignorage by way of interest, considerably exceeds two hundred millions of dollars. If this subsidy of law, depended upon actual service rendered, and not on arbitrary law, it would not probably exceed ten millions of dollars.

The National bank and bond system of the United States can only justly be viewed as a culmination of nearly a hundred years of English banking brigandage under State laws into the largest and most centralized money despotism, the world has ever beheld. The model for this system is purely English, but rich as her history is in every form of tyranny and oppression, she has never dared attempt to carry out such an atrocious system as ours, at anything more than half the rates and upon a minia-ture scale. When therefore, the executive of this nation declares, that " national honor " requires that " every dollar of government indebtedness shall be paid in gold, unless otherwise expressly stipulated in the contract," it is an unequivocal decla-ration for an exterminating war upon the rights of the labor classes. It is not merely a premium offered to the belligerent doctrine, gold- gambling and stock-jobbing dignitaries of the old world; but it contains a scathing rebuke to any claim of rights for the toilers who pay every dollar of this debt. It gives point and force to the almost prophetic declaration of William Pitt, the great English statesman who said : " Let the Ameri-cans adopt their funding system, and go into their banking institutions, and their boasted independence will be a mere phantom." That day has at length arrived when the Americans have gone into their funding and banking systems. The decree has also gone forth that financiers whether native or foreign, are to be paid six per cent gold interest, and one hundred dollars gold for every forty furnished by them. Henceforth too London stock-boards are to be the seat of Government for the great

American Republic. There the annual fruits of American industry are to be gathered and "worthless rags" converted into solid gold.

It is difficult to present any adequate idea of the evils which must flow from this gigantic false paper-money and bond monopoly. To the American mind, it does not seem possible, that such immense natural resources can annually be absorbed, and yet that each succeeding year shall bring an increased demand.

Under the State system, if the bank broke, the loss could be pocketed, and there the wrong ended, but under this paper converted into bonds, the two hundred millions of dollars annual interest, are a perpetual draft upon labor which can never be satisfied.

Any comparison therefore, or any lesson which can be drawn from the past history of banking in this country will give but a faint idea of the rapid centralization of wealth, and the depletion of the many, which must inevitably flow from this fruitful source of oppression and wrong.

The old Alchymists tried in vain to discover a process whereby every thing could be transmuted into gold, but it was left to American statesmen through the banker's gold rimmed spectacles to discover a mode whereby the national laboratory can transmute everything into gold, not even excepting banker's wild cat promises. While their granaries and vaults are being filled by this National class legislation, they seem to think that it is astonishing that their system can be thought otherwise than universally beneficial. Institutions to which men have been accustomed, however wrong and absurd, come at length to be considered as necessary to social order, and the well-being of the State. Hence, as long as evils are, or can be tolerated, men are disposed to bear up under them as incurable. Say, in his work on Political Economy, speaking upon this subject observes that "certain individuals who have never caught a glympse of a more improved state of society, boldly affirm that it cannot exist, they acquiesce in established evils, and console themselves for their existence by remarking that they could not posssibly be otherwise—in this respect reminding us of the Emperor of Japan, who thought he should have been suffocated with laughter on hearing that the Dutch had no King. The Iroquois were at a loss to conceive, how wars could be carried on with success, if prisoners were not to be burnt."

That a rightly instituted paper-money under governmental control would be much cheaper and better than coin there is no doubt. Even currrency unjustly instituted for the purposes of private gain has in every civilized nation practically taken the place of coin for the last hundred years. But are we as a people therefore, so indissolubly wedded to this state-paper-labor-plundering system, that we are willing to perpetuate it as the great essential element of National power, as a perpetual boon granted to financiers for their benevolent guardianship of the rights and property of the people. Do we really believe that the labor-classes ought to pay to these faithful custodians of government and people over $200,000,000 per annum interest, or rent, for furnishing paper tallies, or counters, in the exchange of the annual productions of the nation. That such a system will produce a fluctuating market for stocks and property is certain. That we may thereby build up a vast gold-speculating, stock-jobbing money monopoly and despotism, which will make our "boasted independence a phantom," is shown by the unjust principles which lie at its base.

If anything more is needed to establish this fact beyond the power of controversy, it can be found in the history of American banking, and its great prototype and exemplar the Bank of England.

No nation has ever come within the range of this English bond and money system, which has not found it a mill-stone around the neck of labor which cannot be lifted. The Ultima Thule of the system is a centralized government, a relentless purse proud and heartless aristocracy, supported and sustained by class law, and an utter and hopeless pauperization of labor. These results are as sure to follow the continuation of this system as death is to follow as the appointed lot of every human being. The only outlet and pathway of safety to the labor classes is the abolishment of coinage, gold bonds and banking, a reduction of interest at least two-thirds, the establishment of money based upon property, at rates not exceeding its cost, and under direct governmental supervision and control.

CHAPTER XII.

IRREDEEMABLE CURRENCIES.

The wrongs of banking are nowhere so speedily and so extensively manifested as in some great national calamity. Let war sweep its desolating course over the country, and thereby disturb its productive industries, then in proportion to the wide spread desolation will be the exacting demands of the financial classes.

While the industrial population freely sacrifice their lives and their fortunes, capitalists are benignly devising ways and means, to make the greater gains out of their country's misfortunes. Having previously shaped the financial legislation and thereby controlled the exchanges, they are easily enabled to accomplish this end. An increased demand of staple articles for consumption, is sure largely to increase the price, an increase of price at once enlarges the demand for the accustomed medium of exchange—this supply being by governmental abdication a monopoly in the hands of the financiers and bankers, they at once commence an organized and systematic course of extortion. Its magnitude is proportioned or moderated only by the exigencies of government and people. What is lacking in previous laws, will soon be supplied by fresh legislation under their dictation. As the land is drenched in blood, their gains will be increased. At the present day the settled line of policy is to exhaust the small supply of currency which is easily done. Then a resort is made to the manufacture of interest bearing bonds to be sold in market at such prices as shall be settled upon by the tender consciences of these licensed plunderers of the people—the so-called capitalists.

Formerly a forced loan was made at the point of the bayonet, or some species of revenues, or property was pledged for the redemption of these issues, or for their payment. Of this character were the issues of the assignats of France—they were in legal effect a sort of French bond and mortgage combined, whereby an individual interest in the forfeited church-estates was pledge as the funds for the redemption of the obligations, or as its only base, the bond was substantially in the following form:

Law of 25 May, 1793	Republic of France	FIFTEEN SOUS	One and Indivisible	The 2d year of the Republic

NATIONAL DOMAIN.

FIFTFEN CENT BOND

PAYABLE TO BEARER.

GERARD.   FEGUET.

BUTTIN.

SERIES.   1552.

FIFTEEN, XV SOUS.

The Law punishes with Death the 'Counterfeiter.	**15s**	The Nation will recompense the Informer.

The French National Assembly having appropriated the Church Estates to national purposes, instead of throwing the land upon the market when its value was so largely depreciated, issued these bonds called "Assignats," which represented the land as assigned to the holder. These bonds were principally for 100 francs, (£4) each. Though some were issued as low as ten or five francs and even lower. The first issue was 400 million francs, these were issued in the spring of 1790, and bore interest but subsequent issues did not. This system once inaugurated was afterwards repeatedly applied to the property of wealthy persons who abandoned their country and whose estates were confiscated by the State. Assignats based on these forfeitures were issued until they reached the enormous amount of 45,578 million of francs. Besides the country was flooded with forged Assignats manufactured abroad, under such circumstances the value of these securities soon began to decline. In June

1793, one silver franc was worth three in paper, and in August, six. The state applied the usual legislative penalty appliances to compel acceptance at their full nominal value, but of course this expedient failed in a country where the kings had taught the people to worship only gold, and where untold misery had been produced by the Mississippi Bubble Act of John Law, based upon cotton plantations, to be planted in the then wilderness of Louisiana, and upon ship loads of prostitutes shipped from Paris to people that delightful French Paradise. With such a prelude it was not likely that pains and penalties could give a money credit to a most baseless and credit destroyed bond— especially when the populace had already shouldered the loss. A few wealthy sharks had enriched themselves by purchasing the bonds for a trifle, and thereby obtained the lands which these bonds represented. In March 1776, a Louis d'or (24 francs) brought 7,200 francs in "Assignats," during this year the government substituted the mandats, a new paper-issue, by which the Assignats were redeemed at $\frac{1}{30}$th their nominal value. These mandats were convertible into public lands at their estimated value and the holder could enter into possession at once, while the Assignat was an undivided interest in the land which could only be realized by public sale. A law passed in 1796, restored business to its ancient channels by leaving every one to transact business in such medium as he chose, providing also that mandats should be taken at their current value, and taxes received either in coin, or mandats at that rate. Thus ended the reign of Assignats in France.

The Mississippi Bubble Act of John Law—the Assignats of France and Russia—the continental coin obligations of the United States, and all other similar paper-issues have not the least tendency to show whether a good paper-money can or cannot be issued by the government. These paper-issues should be viewed as the direct result of imperfect and unjust laws instituted in times of great public peril, and all of them based upon the extremely unjust class ideas out of which all government-bonds, money and currency have so far originated. All taken together are designed to benefit a ruling or controlling class by creating unjust and arbitrary gains largely in excess of the natural rewards of productive industry.

In these laws is truly verified the declaration that when the wicked rule the land mourneth. How more grave injustice, or gross inequality of distribution of property can be compressed into a legislative enactment than is included in this whole financial system, is as yet undiscovered? Why these revolutionary land and coin bonds should be denominated an "irredeemable currency," any more than the money and currency out of which they originated, cannot well be explained. These bonds were never redeemed, and no banker's currency has ever yet been instituted which has been truly a redeemable currency. The latter answers in sunshine, but both perish in a storm. The former have defrauded the masses out of a few hundred millions, the latter out of as many thousands of millions. They should all be branded as "irredeemable currencies," originating in such barbarism and despotism, that they ought no longer to disgrace the statute books of a free and enlightened people. The great industrial classes although they may not be able to trace these evils back to their source, they know full well that they are grossly wronged by the system, and the greenback was the nearest approach to a correct system of anything yet attempted in legislation—they therefore justly desire to retain this money, and to get rid of the National bankers, they do not see the propriety of paying two interests, when one is twice what it ought to be, and more than twice what it is, in the despotic countries of Europe. Republican governments should not duplicate the bad deeds of European despots. Such roses do not render a sweet perfume, though christened Democratic or Republican.

CHAPTER XIII.

ELASTICITY AND CONVERTIBILITY.

Elasticity and convertibility are enigmatical terms designed and used by financiers to cover up some of the gross iniquities of banking.. Elasticity is thus happily described by one imaginative financial writer in the banking interest. He says: "The value of a bank medium consists in its elasticity—in its power of ultimate expansion and contraction to suit the wants of the community—in truth the merit of a bank medium is nearly in proportion to the flexibility of its means." Unfortunately for the truth of this beautiful theory, bank flexibility and business wants, generally run in counter directions. When business demands increased facilities, the inexorable banker's interest demands a rigid contraction.

Convertibility ostensibly denotes coin redemption at the will of the holder—but practically it denotes a will that must never be exercised in that direction, without a certain and inevitable defeat.

At the present time the use of these two terms are designed to pave the way for the destruction of the "greenback"—the ushering in of a plentiful supply of gold interest bonds, and to secure the absolute and unconditional supremacy of the so-called National-banking.

Capitalists who have made millions upon millions of dollars in the issue of the worst species of a non-elastic and non-redeemable currency, are suddenly seized with an epidemic, if not a contagious gold convertible fever—they are horrified at the shocking depreciation of a non-convertible, irredeemable governmental paper-money. What a monstrosity? Having converted a much worse class of an unsecured, no interest bearing currency into the people's property—then with large interest and profits added, converted it back again into a six per cent. interest bearing gold bond. If they can now convert the balance of the "greenbacks" into the same class of bonds into which they have previously funded their irredeemable wild cat trash, it will constitute the banker's paradise regained.

Yet, in their eagerness to reach these paradisaical joys, if they should omit to mention the important fact—it will be well for us at least, to remember, that the greenback is now lawful money for all purposes but two—interest on the public debt and impost duties—for this unjust discrimination against labor and in favor of the capitalists—— to them the country is principally indebted for this National discredit of the greenback.

Patriotism is said to be that unselfish and hallowed feeling of disinterestedness, which freely sacrifises property and life if need be, for the good of one's country. A patriotism and love of country so puré as wholly to leave out selfhood, cannot take filthy lucre in. But that patriotism which influenced the capitalists to take part in our late fratricidal contest was one which left the widest margin for profits. When they found that the ignoble many were placed between them and danger and that they could control the National financial legislation solely for their own gain, their patriotism then knew no bounds. Yet it does not however seem to be a patriotism of a very exalted character, or one that augurs so much good for the people, that its kindly offices should be accepted without qualification or enquiry.

Like the serpent, it whispers in our ears of the good time coming, when gold shall reign supreme; besides that it is "pleasant to behold, and good for food." But alas! the smiling invitation and cheering promises are delusive. If we hear not the prophetic declaration "that in the day thou eatest thereof, thou shalt surely die." It is nevertheless true, there is death in the bowl—death to political, civil and religious liberty.

Let no one be deceived by these *gold-base* pretensions—no gold base, gold bonds, nor bankers redeemable currency can fill up the terrible chasm of a four years war—they may load down the productive industry of the country with the overwhelming burthens of their oppressive system, but no concessions will be made to the people which does not bring to the financiers a greater private gain.

But when these oppressive burdens, and their attendant evils become almost insupportable. When the public mind is beginning in earnest to enquire into the causes of these grievous wrongs; the financiers, politicians, public journals, political, commercial and even the religious press are not exempt from the contagion, of delivering homiletics upon national honor. This demands at the bidding of the capitalists, an unconditional surrender of the rights of the people, and teaches that genuine honesty and an untarnished public faith requires the payment of a financier's forty per cent. national paper debt, in a people's hundred per cent. interest bearing gold bond. Learned dissertations too are written by savans and political economists, to prove that this mode of extortion with a gold-base, and under the financiers' control, are all that is needed to give elasticity and convertibility to the banker's national currency.

Now it is well known that all the industrial and useful classes desire, is a just and equitable adjustment of the National debt, and an honest, safe and uniform medium of exchange at actual cost. As they furnished all the values and did and do, all the actual, useful business, they certainly have a right to demand this much from the government. But this demand should not be met by licensing hordes of foreign and home gold speculators, stock-jobbers, and bankers to plunder them.

How can "elasticity" and "convertibility" be permanently attained, or how can the people be benefitted or secured their rights, under a system, which, while it establishes a double and high interest, requires a correspondingly decreased price of products to support it. Under such a system what is not reached by discounts or by interest, must be absorbed by brokerage. Hence every large banking establishment includes in it these two elements—discounts and brokerage—profits from discounts made, while trade is being stimulated by excessive paper-issues, are endurable only in anticipation of a greater harvest of depreciated property by brokerage. Burdens are thus stored by law for the people, and increased benefits for the capitalists. How can anything else but evil flow from such a system. As we have repeatedly shown, it is not gold or silver, not even the capital of the stockholders which enables them to redeem their notes, but it is the avails of the people's property through the artificial channels of trade thus arbitrarily and unjustly created by National and State financial laws.

Whenever therefore there is a large increase of staples with an increased foreign demand, the banks immediately expand their issues, speculations soon becomes rife, bank-paper is its natural element. Increased demand raises prices, and the high price of products, increases the price of labor. Then manufactured goods, and every other commodity experiences a proportionate rise, until at length the home demand cuts off the foreign, and what little was gained by that demand is absorbed in interest and profits which through this bank medium is gathered into a few hands. Thus the great productive industry of the country is on the whole injured more than benefitted, especially that of the middle and lower classes of labor. These depend upon labor entirely for their support. Increase of prices by these means are generally first and highest on manufactured goods—products last—and the same observations apply to the whole routine of labor and business. The boasted elasticity of the currency never operates any other way. It is perfectly immaterial from what stand-point the subject is viewed. It is false to the interests of the people, in its origin, principles and results.

That the governmental land monopolist and feudal baron of Europe, could see nothing valuable but in lands, bonds, gold and silver is not strange. His grandeur and his power was sustained by it. Hence he fostered every device which increased these, and was jealous of that which might impair his seignory, or reduce his substantial wealth in lands, silver and gold. But the state in support of these not unfrequently exorbitant claims of royalty was frequently obliged to anticipate their annual tax or tithe in advance by representatives of paper. Hence two other classes began to sssume importance in the civil state, dealers in stocks and other representatives of value, and the world's traders. Side by side these several classes grew up and were fostered and fed not by labor, not for services rendered, but by prerogatives of State. The first by land and governmental monopoly. The two latter classes, stock-jobbers and traders became its purveyors—one sought governmental ' stocks and grants—the other by them commercial facilities.

Hence the governmental land monopoly class and their retainers, seeing the substantial character of the land and gold monopoly, naturally became bullionists—this to them never depreciated. But the dealers in paper and gold lived on the substantial shadows of land and gold, in representatives, which drew interest, or afforded profits.

But even bonds and other securities when they brought the

gold and silver to the bullionists were substantial—when they demanded these, beyond their power of supply, then these pictured classes of wealth were unsubstantial and unreal. But all these classes agreed in this, that the difference or losses must be taken out of labor. The governmental and banking class charge the wrong to over-trading. Over-traders charge it back to bad financial laws and want of gold. One class claims that gold and silver are the only reliable currency. The other that a "gold-base," convertible "currency" is all that is desirable. But all agree that whether a gold-base, or gold, it must be reached through the strong arms of labor. Thus between these classes, bullion and anti-bullion, gold-base, or by an elastic, gold convertible currency the rights of the masses are ground to powder.

The bullionists robs by a monopoly of gold, and the anti-bullionists by his gold interest bond and gold-base currency, but so far as speculation is concerned, the bullionist-theory has the advantage of the paper-theorists. So long as exchanges are made in gold, there is no danger of serious over-speculation at home or abroad. Trade in barter is a *quid pro quo* transaction —this thing for that—and there is not much chance for excess or loss.

If the barter trade fails that ends the injury—the evil is not aggravated by failures of money, or currency based on that trade.

Even wars and legalized governmental robberies by gold do not create a demand for gold for home consumption beyond the supply. The pressure only comes to meet the foreign demand— it is not two-fold, the one to meet the demand of a gold-base law, the other to meet the foreign demand, for that has already been met.

If there is a demand for staples abroad, the prices at home will not be suddenly enhanced by an increase of the currency, so as to destroy the advantage of the exportation, and thus make it a losing business.

These are some of the advantages claimed for an inflexible non-elastic gold-money. As against the elastics on the score of honesty and uniformity of value, the "non-elastics" or bullionists have the advantage.

Both systems however are an odious monopoly. Gold as money is too expensive. Although paper-money can be furnished at one-eighth the cost of coin, yet under this bank regime, it is even more expensive. Losses by insolvency, exorbitant rates of interest, an irregular supply and constant derangement of business, makes it a most expensive luxury—the gold-base furnishes an apology for extortionate interest. If the gold was actually kept on hand, then the public are entirely deprived of its use. Thus the use of the coin is a dead loss, and the cost of the paper-issue, is just that much excess of expense, over what it would cost to circulate the coin.

A paper medium therefore, which legally and honestly denotes the commodities exchanged under government control, without having to pass through this dishonest gold-base circumlocution office would not cost exceeding one-eighth of the present cost of currency and coin.

One million dollars worth of wheat, furnishes as good a base as coin, for all the money required in exchanging that amount of property in the ordinary channels of trade. The wheat equally with gold is a property base, and the grain on the principle proposed is not diverted from its natural use in supplying the wants of man—Whereas the gold if a fund for the redemption of the money, is so much value, miser-like, withdrawn from its appropriate sphere of use. But in truth no currency or money is erected on a gold base—practically, money or currency, denotes the property sold or exchanged. It is both a certificate of value of the property or service furnished or rendered and a legal order for the amount of property thereby indicated, subject to payment of the cost of production which is determined by the market price of the article.

To illustrate this. Suppose the West has one million dollars of wheat which she desires to exchange for one millions dollars worth of Eastern goods. The West takes from the wheat purchasers the wheat paper-money, and the east takes the money for the goods and exchanges the money for the wheat. The West gets the goods and the East gets the wheat. The account between the two sections of country and the respective parties, is balanced through the medium of the wheat-money. No gold or silver is required to give value to this wheat paper-money. Storing up gold therefore, and attempting to connect the money with it, if actually done, would be a useless expense—if it is not done the pretence is an outrageous fraud.

The latter is generally the result—connecting gold or silver with paper-money as the only fund for redemption, under any and every form, has ever been and must continue to be, a potent agency for deranging business, and thereby it has proved a most effective instrument of wrong and oppression.

But to illustrate this elastic gold-convertible money theory and its operation, as connected with foreign commerce—let it be supposed that the United States have had a plentiful harvest this year—the bankers and dealers are eager for the trade. Money is plenty at low rates of interest. Trade soon becomes unnaturally stimulated. Unusual bank facilities are the sure forerunner of vast commercial enterprises at home and abroad. The same principles govern all branches of trade. Exchange to be useful must be mutual. Articles not desired, must pay for those which are needed, and at the least expense. To effect this however, shipments and transhipments may be necessary. Yet each branch of business should be made to furnish its own appropriate medium of exchange—at least the home trade should not unnecessarily through its money medium interfere or derange the foreign trade, neither should the foreign trade be permitted through this same medium, to interfere with, or derange the home industries and exchanges.

Such being the financial and commercial laws which ought to govern, no violation of these fundamental principles of justice can be tolerated with impunity.

If then A. B. and C., being supposed to represent the importers, through National and State bonds, or some of the other devices necessary to support this gold-base system, should import $12,000,000 more goods than could be paid for with exports, then paper-money must supply the coin or bullion to pay the deficit. This demand might occasion a contraction of the currency $60, or $70,000,000. Hence a financial crash would inevitably ensue which would spread disaster and ruin broadcast throughout the land.

We have put this case upon hypothetical grounds, but the financial history of this country and of England is teeming with facts condemnatory of the whole system much stronger than anything here presented.

The crash of 1857 sheds much further light upon this question. Colwell in his book on " the ways and means of payment," thus presents this subject. He says, " Our banks are so constituted, that when the ignorant and alarmed multitude commence a run

for coins, they have no resource but to withdraw the usual facilities of banking from the very men of business to whose custom
they owe all their profits, and to whose forbearance they owe
every day's existence. When this race begins, the banks,
whilst they are daily receiving, in their own notes and credits,
(checks on deposits,) the sums payable to them, withhold the
customary facilities or discounts from their customers, and by
this means create such a strong demand for bank-notes and credits for payment of debts as checks their presentation for specie.
The stream of bank-notes and deposits sets strongly and steadily
towards the banks, and returns to the public in a constantly
decreasing volume. The demand of the banks upon the public
may continue unabated for some sixty days, in which time in a
commercial community, the stringency may become such, that
few, if any, can have bank-notes or credits upon which to make
demand for specie, and those who have, will be tempted by the
debtors to the banks to accept at the rate of twelve, eighteen,
twenty, or thirty per cent. per annum; and thus these bank-
notes and bank credits will be returned to the banks in payment
of debts, in place of being presented for payment in specie.
The contraction in New York, in the panic of 1857, is a specimen of what the banks are constrained to do to save themselves.
They can only protect their coffers by refusing to issue the usual
supply of currency. The diminution of loans and deposits in
the banks of New York City, stood thus in August and October,
1857 :

	Loans.	Deposits.
15th of August....	$121,241,472....	$92,356,328
19th of September..	108,777,421....	75,772,774
17th of October...	97,245,826....	52,894,623

This exhibits a reduction of discounts, in one month of
$13,000,000, and in the succeeding month of $11,000,000; that
is $24,000,000 in sixty days; in one month deposits ran down
under this operation, $17,000,000; in the succeeding month,
$23,000,000; making in the two months a reduction in the chief
medium of payment of $40,000,000. Deposits were thus reduced
nearly one-half. It cannot be surprising that under such a process of contraction, interest went up to between fifteen and
thirty-six per cent., and exchange down to nine or ten per cent.
below par. What the banks did in New York, was done in a
greater or less degree in other cities; bankruptcy, ruin and
destruction followed. It is estimated that from five to six

thousand failures occurred, involving an indebtedness of from $280,000,000 to $300,000,000 with a loss to creditors of more than $150,000,000. But this loss bears no comparison with that arising from the depreciation of securities, and from the fall in price of real and personal property, which, judging from the results of estimates carefully made, cannot be less than $500,000,000, and may not improbably be twice that sum. The loss sustained by the men who labor for their living is even more severe in its consequences, if not equal in pecuniary amount. A million of men idle for six months involves a loss upon the machinery, shops, tools and factories, which stand idle when the workmen are unemployed.

The late panic has inflicted, in all its bearings and ramifications, a loss upon the country which is variously estimated from $500,000,000 to $1,000,000,000. No doubt the ill-effects of the panic were much enhanced by the previous abuse of credit, and that a considerable portion of this devastation should be set down to that account. With every allowance in that respect, we shall have a vast sum of loss to charge to the panic ; and whether this sum be $400,000,000 or $800,000,000, matters not to our view. The loss was, to a great extent, unnecessary, cruel, terrible—a loss which has carried privation, distress and ruin to a million of homes. For a time, at least, not yet passed, it reduced hundreds of thousands of the best people to a state of entire dependence, if not beggary.

What was the occasion of these dire calamities? The banks of the United States had a reserve of specie for several years previous to 1857, and during the first half of that year, amounting to somewhat over $50,000,000 ; and of this, the banks of the City of New York held a little more than one-fifth. To save this amount of specie, the banks contracted the currency one-half, denied the usual facilities upon their books, put up the rate of interest from twelve to thirty-six per cent., put down exchange upon England to nine or ten per cent. below par, reduced the revenue from customs to less than half of the usual amount, drew a surplus of $20,000,000 of gold out of the public treasury, and drove the government to an issue of paper promises to pay its current expenses, deprived hundreds of thousands, perhaps of their customary employment, caused some five or six thousand failures among men of business, and finally inflicted a loss on the country, in the depreciation of securities, in the reduction of prices and by insolvency, of several hundred millions. Not to save this sum of fifty millions from being lost, sunk in the ocean, or thrown away, were all these encountered, but merely to prevent it from passing into circulation among the people, or at the worst, to prevent it from being exported in payment of debts due in foreign countries. Nine-tenths of the debts of the country are paid, as we have seen, by the agency of discounts and deposits, with some aid from the circulation of the banks; but the banks have been placed under such heavy penalties to pay all their liabilities in specie on demand, that when they are threatened with a panic, a commercial revulsion, or a heavy export of specie to foreign countries, they are compelled, like Samson in the temple of the Philistines, to pull down the whole fabric of credit, public and private, about the ears of the people, to disturb and check the progress of industry in all its departments, to make bankrupts of their customers, and to sow pauperism broadcast in the field of labor.

This compelled policy of the banks, under the stringency of the laws which govern them, has been called paying specie. But with how little propriety. Instead of paying their liabilities with commercial promptness and the faithfulness of those who are discharging a legal and moral obligation, they resist it with all the power and weapons they can command. In the struggles incident to this resistance they strike down friends as well as enemies and deprive the public of an amount of currency necessary to business, ten times greater than the specie they are unwilling to pay out.

And this is the convertibility so long aimed at, and to secure which so much legislation and so much thought has been expended! This is the triumph of banks which pass through a season of panic and revulsion without suspending! a triumph like the victory which leaves 100,000 dead bodies on the field of battle, which makes 10,000 widows, 50,000 orphans, and 200,000 paupers!"

This "elastic convertible gold-base" system, is the one which is proposed as a cure for a pretended "irredeemable and inflated" government money, but which is in fact a good money. Though the country is suffering considerably under the effects produced from a long and bloody war, very largely increased by the extortions and other iniquities practiced upon government and people, by the financiers and bankers through this wicked financial system; yet with all these accumulated evils upon the nation, the "greenback" carried the government triumphantly through the war, and to-day honestly marks the price of products increased in the cost of production, by the losses occasioned by war, and by the greater robbery perpetrated upon the nation by these very financiers and bankers.

Whenever the people therefore consent to surrender the entire money-power of the government into the hands of this Philistine crew of "capitalists," to the destruction or gold interest funding of the "legal tenders, and to the perfecting of the organization of the present National Banking system—then surely we shall need no blind Samson to pull down the pillars of Freedom's consecrated temple, for we shall have effectually accomplished that suicidal work with our own hands—that dread alternative is even now awaiting the decision of the American people.

It is not "convertibility," it is not a "gold-base," nor a reliable money for which these men are clamoring, but it is for the supreme control of the government through a bonded and money system assimilated as near as possible to that of the Bank and bond system of England.

CHAPTER XIV.

INTEREST ON MONEY.

Interest is the sum paid for what is technically called the use of money. The origin of this term as applied to this charge, it might be difficult to ascertain, and if ascertained the knowledge would not probably be very useful. For a long period of time it was denominated usury. The Hebrew word *nashach*, which we translate usury, means to bite as a serpent, and in psalms Chap. XV., 5 verse it is said that "he that putteth not out his money to usury nor taketh reward against the innocent. He that doeth these things shall never be moved,' upon which text the commentator remarks that "here *nashac* must signify that biting, or devouring usury, which ruins the man who has it to pay." "The increase of usury is called *neshec*, because it resembles the biting of a serpent. For as this is so small at first as scarcely to be perceptible, but the venom soon spreads and diffuses itself till it reaches the vitals: So the increase of usury which at first is not perceived, nor felt, at length grows so much as by degrees to devour another's substance." Middoch's Ed. of Leigh's Critica Sacra Sub voce—Nashach—Adam Clark's Comm's.

Dr. Clark confines the term usury to excess of interest, but all interest between Jews was unlawful, they were only allowed to charge interest or rent to strangers. There was substantial justice in this law—he, being a member of the commonwealth of Israel was obliged to pay his full share of expenses for protection to property and life, and was thus entitled without further charge to enjoy all the blessings of the social, religious and civil order—but with the stranger or gentile it was otherwise—he might enjoy these for a rent, but even to him extortionate excess of charge, was not allowable.

The Church in its infancy prohibited usury, and good men in every age of the world, have not failed to lift their voices against it, but the state has legalized certain rates as "interest" and anathematized any excess over those rates as usury, under this salvo of state, the consciences of a great many pious men are quieted, and are frequently not disturbed with any usury, where the interest does not exceed two or three per cent. per month. The right at least to receive the legal rate, of from six to ten per cent. interest, is generally unchallenged in this country. Thus it is seen how easily the voice of reason and conscience is stifled, and the revealed, as well as the natural law, is made void by human statutes and human traditions.

But among all the grave crimes that governments and despots have committed, there is none which in enormity and extent, can compare with the wrongs inflicted upon mankind by the establishment of usury, or "interest." The legal distinction between interest and usury, is an Alexandrine one—it is a dividing line between petit larceny and robbery. No good reason can be given it is apprehended why in justice and equity, interest should be lawful, and usury unlawful. Neither has any reference to a just compensation.

It may be laid down as an axiom in the science of political economy, that each person in the body politic, is entitled to that portion in the distribution of the annual productions, that his mental and physical labor has added to the common stock, or contributed to the general welfare of the State. Equally true is it, that governments are instituted among men, for the purpose of securing domestic tranquility in the establishment of just and equal laws, and the most essential or fundamental law in any nation, is that which institutes money. For by it labor is rewarded and property distributed. If then there is any inequality or injustice in the law instituting money, it invades with injustice every transaction in business, and this injustice increases in a geometrical ratio in every transaction—subsequent to the first.

Kellogg, in his New Monetary system claims, that "there are only two purposes to which the yearly products of labor can be applied." One is the payment of the yearly rent or interest on the capital employed, and the other is the payment of labor." That "the law of interest, or percentage on money, as much governs the rent or use of all property, and consequently the reward of labor, as the law of gravitation governs the descent of water." He further says that " with the present accumulative power of interest,'there is no more chance of the laboring classes gaining their rights by combining their labor to increase production, than there would be hope of success that by combining their labor they could reverse the course of the rivers, and make them run to the tops of the mountains, and pile up the water on their summits. The law of gravitation, in the latter case, would not be more sure to overpower all their labor, and frustrate all their plans, than the present governing power of the interest on money, is sure to gather up the increased production, and add it to the wealth of capitalists. The fault is in the law which governs the distribution of property; and combinations to increase production would no more effect any general change in the distribution, than combinations against the law of gravitation would effect a change in its general governing powers. The evil is legislative, and the remedy must be legislative." And Mr. Campbell has shown in his "True American System" that putting the population of the United States in 1790, at 4,000,000, and the property at $1,000,000,000—this sum loaned at eight per cent. per annum interest for seventy years would amount to $54,639,310,642. This shows the gross injustice of this system of distribution and the utter impossibility there is in attempting to meet by any exertion of physical labor, the demands of such an iniquitous law, or to secure under it by mere labor anything more than a scanty pittance of one's annual earnings.

If we descend into particulars the enormity of this wrong is made still more apparent. In 1856, the banks of the United States, loaned as appears from their reports, $684,000,000, this at six per cent. interest would be upwards of $41,000,000. How much business was done outside the banks cannot easily be ascertained, but taking the average rate of interest to be ten per cent., and the amount of discount and interest paid outside of bank deals would probably exceed $68,000,000. So that the whole sum paid for 1856, must exceed $100,000,000.

For the year 1857, the clearings of the New York clearing house were about $7,196,000,000. If this sum drew on an average two months interest, and under the revulsion fifteen per cent., it would amount to over $71,000,000 in New York City alone. Taking the whole United States, it is a very moderate estimate to place it at $450,000,000. Able financiers have put it as high as $900,000,000—at the present time the amount would exceed $1,000,000000, but $550,000,000 will not reach the amount paid. The interest on the government debt last year was some $137,000,000, and for the next year it is estimated that it will reach $145,000,000. If then the wrong consisted in the inequality of the law, simply and in awarding so high a rate of rent, we should have no hesitancy in declaring it one of the most grievous wrongs which could well be inflicted upon the masses.

The objection however to the payment of interest does not rest upon the ground of its excessive amount alone, but it is based upon the more substantial principle, that the requirement to pay interest, or any sum above the governmental cost, is a direct violation of the first and most essential principle of government and of right.

The issuing of money and all its substitutes is the exercise of a governmental power the highest known. No power but the sovereign power, is adequate to the institution of money. No individual, nor any number of them short of those constituting the sovereign power, are competent to say what shall be money, and how it shall be instituted, what are to be its functions, or how it shall be regulated or controlled. These are questions which must be authoritatively settled by the supreme power of the State—the unfaithful exercise of this power, or its total abandonment and entire abdication, does not destroy the right, or excuse those who have violated this solemn duty.

We have seen that the only fund used for the redemption of a currency, is the avails of the property purchased, the furnishing and regulating of the medium, is as much a matter of governmental control, as is coinage or the instituting a court; and to make laws granting out this power to corporations or to individuals, and fixing tolls and other regulations, is simply letting out the governmental power, for private use, and private gain—the leasing out of Congress, the Army, Navy, or Judiciary, would be no more a gross violation of governmental rights, and of governmental duties.

The origin of this system like the cumbrous and unjust modes of taxation, is barbarism and despotism. Custom or usage has so far obscured the spoilation of the people's rights, that the yoke is rendered easy, and the burden light. We do not stop to enquire until a failure of crops, a financial crash, or fell war's hellish scenes obliges us to lift the curtain, and behold the hideous deformity and rottenness of the whole system. What else, but blindfold custom could make the people willing to pay some

$900,000,000 or perhaps $1,000,000,000, in the annual exchange of their products of $1,500,000,000, when the whole cost to the capitalists are simply the complicated, legalized tallies or counters of the property—or what else could make them willing to pay between $7,000, and $8,000, in assessing, collecting, storing and furnishing the circulating medium to pay the President a salary of $25,000, and all other officers and public expenditures at the same rate. The government could, and would under a rightly instituted system like the greenback, pay that sum and not cost per annum exceeding $250.

In making this estimate of $900,000,000, or $1,000,000,000 per annum interest—the whole range of interest on notes, bonds, accounts and all classes of dealing with the discounts of notes by bankers and other dealers are included. The single item of discounts or interest on the money, and on the public debt, will as hereinbefore stated, exceed $200,000,000, that was confined exclusively to the items named, whereas this last estimate includes the annual deranging, cumulative power of interest in every department of business and trade, and which may be justly chargeable to the unjust mode of instituting money, and the establishment of interest by National and State laws.

CHAPTER XV.

PREMIUMS ON GOLD.

The theories respecting premiums on gold, and the depreciation of paper-money from over-issues as shown by increased
prices, whether of products or gold, like our paper-money system
are a precious morceau of British manufacture, out of which the
American people are making themselves exceedingly rich; by
paying for these valuable paper-theories an enormous tariff in
solid gold. The only abatement or loss on our side of the
balance sheet is found to be, that the British pile up gold, by
way of our interest bonds, and we pile up gold bonds by way of
interest. But as the labor class must earn it, and we have plenty
of wild lands, gold mines, and other like things which England
desires, the difference between a loss to us, and their gain is only
a few billions of dollars, which is so trifling a matter that we
cannot afford to lose the good opinion of the British Aristocrats,
by daring to enquire into the soundness of their theories, or the
justice of their demands arising under the operation of those
theories.

The author of money in the Encyclopedia Britannica says:
"The premium' on gold in 1814 is an indigestible fact for those
who contend that bank-notes being issued in proportion to the
demand, have not been depreciated from excessive issues." Yet
the history of the British paper-money like our greenback, under
precisely similar circumstances, furnishes a full and complete
refutation of this encyclopediast's position, but the objects of the
British financiers like that of ours, being by legislation to take
the difference, or loss out of the people in gold, through gold
interest bonds, the truth could not be perceived by them, any
more than it can by those at home and abroad who desire to
plunder us by the same means, and to a much worse extent.

The following are the facts as shown by the tables of the

British market during the years named. From 1809 to 1810, increased circulation of paper-money twenty per cent. premiums on gold *fell* seven per cent., from 1810 to 1811 the increase of the circulation was two per cent., while the premium on gold rose 15½ per cent.; from 1811 to 1813, increase of circulation three per cent., increased premium on gold eleven and a half per cent; from 1813 to 1814, increase of circulation ten per cent., premium on gold fell six per cent.; from 1814 to 1815, circulation increased nearly three per cent., premium on gold fell eleven per cent.; from 1815 to 1816, circulation decreased over one per cent., premium on gold fell sixteen and a half per cent.; from 1816 to 1817, circulation increased five per cent., premium on gold same as in 1816; in 1818 decrease of circulation over five per cent., premium on gold more than doubled. In 1819 decrease of circulation eight per cent. premium on gold, rose over one per cent. If Encyclopediast or any one else maintaining the British gold regulating, and currency inflation theories; can find anything in these facts to show that there was any connection between the increased circulation and the premium on gold, there would be at least some excuse for the wholesale slaughter of business by currency contraction.

Mr. Tooke in his work on prices, gives the following explanation of the fluctuations of prices in the British market during the period above described. He says, " the relatively high prices of articles in the interval from 1793 to 1814, may be ascribed to the following general circumstances :"

" 1. The frequent recurrence of seasons of an unfavorable character—there having been in that interval no fewer than eleven seasons in which the general produce of corn, but more especially of wheat was deficient.

" 2. The destruction of a great source of supply of transatlantic produce by the revolution in St. Domingo, which rendered sugar and coffee and most other West India produce scarce and dear during the earlier part of the war.

" 3. Obstructions and prohibitions of export from the continent of Europe of articles of which whether as raw materials of our manufactures, or naval stores, or food we stood in urgent need.

" 4. Increased cost of transportation, by higher freights and insurance incidental to a state of war, generally aggravated by the peculiar commercial hostility and exclusion which marked the latter years.

"5. The difference of exchange which in the last five years of the war averaged twenty per cent.

" 6. A higher rate of interest, in consequence of the absorption by the war loans, of a considerable proportion of the savings of individuals·"

The causes of the decline, and of the lower range of prices from 1814 to 1837, except 1816–'17, which was a moment of great scarcity over all Europe, were :

1. A succession of more favorable seasons in the last twenty years from 1818, there having been but five seasons in which the produce of wheat was decidedly deficient.

2. The removal of obstacles from the several sources of foreign supply ; a great extension of some of them and the discovery of new ones.

3. A great reduction of the charges of importation by low freights and insurances and the improved and cheaper and more rapid internal communication.

4. A rise in the foreign exchanges, and consequent reduction of the cost of all imported commodities.

5. Improvement in machinery, in chemistry, and in the arts and sciences generally, all tending to reduce the cost of production of numerous articles, or to provide cheaper substitutes.

6. A reduction of the rate of interest.

There is not as far as I have been able to discover, any considerable commodity in the whole range of articles embraced in the most extensive list of prices, the variations of which do not admit of being distinctly accounted for by circumstances peculiar to it, in the relation of supply, actual or contingent, real or apprehended to the ordinary rate of consumption without supposing any influence from the bank restriction beyond the degree in which the difference of exchange, which could not have existed but for the restriction, may be considered to have operated distinctly, on the cost of production."

McCulloch states, " that there is not a single commodity that has fallen in price since 1814, the fall of which may not be satisfactorily accounted for without such reference."

Here then is the solution of British statesmen and savans, showing that the high and constantly fluctuating premium on gold did not originate from currency inflation. Although all that is stated may be and undoubtedly is true—yet it would be strange, if reasons of state did not otherwise control, that the most essential causes, should not have been mentioned.

In 1776, England went into a war with her colonies, now the United States, to tax them without the right of representation; that war was a heavy draft upon the productive industry of that country for men to be sent abroad to fight the battles, as well as for gold to furnish supplies and munitions of war. When these two resources, men and gold failed; for men, she hired the Hessians to do her butchery, and for gold, sold interest bonds at a large discount. From that moment the difficulties of England commenced in earnest—a war with France, followed by a general continental war—a larger demand for men and money, and to pay this, required an interest indebtedness to be largely increased. The large increase of the interest bearing debt, with the decreased supply of labor, for a long time made a constantly increased demand for paper or other money, to denote the corresponding increase of prices thereby created. High prices, and high premiums, were the products of largely increased interest and discounts on money and bonds, added to the difficulties of decreased production. The increase of paper therefore, being actually based on property and not any one species of property, did but make the increased cost of production. The inflation then, was not in the paper-money as money, but as we have seen, in the increased burthens created by interest and discounts. Hence the decreased paper-circulation brought an increased premium on gold with but one exception. The exceptional cases are rung in our ears by the capitalists without mercy. While the rights of the people are thereby held in abeyance, charlatan legislators at the instance of capitalist-knaves, succeed in charging over to the labor-classes the whole burthens and wrongs of this financial legislation in an interest bearing bond, to be made the base of an interest bearing paper-money. Thus the capitalist without service and without right consumes the annual productions of labor. Under this machinery of law and custom, British financiers and liberty crushing despot statesmen have fastened upon the productive industry of England over $4,000,000,000 of rent bearing bonds which really represents that amount of property eat up and destroyed by war, to fasten the iron chains of despotism on her American colonies. Failing in that she brands upon the brow of her labor-population the Cain or vagabond mark of perpetual slavery, to feed a worse vagabond set of aristocrats.

Money loaned at ten per cent., will double in seven years three months and five days; at nine per cent., in eight years and fifteen days; at eight per cent., in nine years and two days; at seven per cent., in ten years, two months, and twenty-six days; at six per cent., in eleven years, ten months, and twenty-one days; at five per cent., in seventeen years and eight months; at three per cent., in twenty-three years, five months and ten days; and at two per cent., in about thirty-five years.

As in the bonded system the bond marks, the amount of what the government had consumed during the year with the interest-increased cost of production added, it is a correct mode of calculation under that system to compound the interest. If then the British debt was $1,000,000,000 in 1780, and it be supposed that the increased price of property by this interest be put at four per cent. per annum, in seventeen years and eight months the bond debt would have been increased to $2,000,000,000; in thirty-five years and four months to $4,000,000,000; and in 1820, forty years, to the enormous sum of $6,153,846,153. The larger portion then of $4,000,000,000, besides what was paid, may justly be viewed as the rich legacy bequeathed to the labor-classes of England by her aristocracy in the base attempt to fasten the iron yoke of despotism upon the American colonies.

The pretence of going down to a gold-base only marked the point where British statesmen thought best to limit the interest burthen which they proposed to fasten around the necks of their labor-subjects—the enactment of such a law simply increased the burthen to the extent of the discount on the paper. It had no tendency to establish a stable currency, but just the contrary. Increasing the value of the bond by such arbitrary enactment did not add to the productive industry of the country one penny, but it did put just that increase into the pocket of the capitalist who held the bond with a double interest and cost of collection to be taken out of the laborer's property that much decreased. Hence this legalized mode of stealing with the double interest device left the labor-classes at the mercy of the capitalist, and either death, or a financial crash every few years is the only way any abatement of their burthens can be obtained.

By the adoption of this British gold-bond, gold-base money-system—the American unnamed nobility have succeded in fastening upon the necks of the labor and *useful* business classes, for the benefit of themselves, and their English, French, and other foreign co-adjutors heavier burthens than King George in his palmiest days of despotism ever dreamed of establishing.

We have thus it is believed fully demonstrated that the funding of the American debt and going down to a gold-base has no tendency to establish a stable currency, but merely largely to increase the burthens of labor, to carry up a paper denominational value by enactment from forty cents to one hundred cents on the dollar—to change a reliable government paper-money based on property, not bearing interest and furnished at cost, to an irredeemable double interest bearing, fluctuating banker's paper-money, falsely pretended to be based on national bonds with perhaps a small percentage of gold. To resist then this European bond-interest-enslaving money system, the people must arouse themselves and put down this despotic money-power, or they are destined ere long to hear the last peal of the funeral dirge of departed liberty.

www.ingramcontent.com/pod-product-compliance
Lightning Source LLC
Chambersburg PA
CBHW030830270326
41928CB00007B/979